FEVER ROAD

A Memoir of Passion and Wanderlust

ERNEST BRAWLEY

All rights reserved. No part of this publication may be reproduced in whole or in part, or stored in a retrieval system, or transmitted in any form or by any means, electronic, mechanical, photocopying, recording, or otherwise, without written permission of the author, except for the inclusion of brief quotations in a review.

Copyright © 2025 by Ernest Brawley

For information regarding permission, please write to:
info@barringerpublishing.com
Barringer Publishing, Naples, Florida
www.barringerpublishing.com

Design and layout by Linda S. Duider
Cape Coral, Florida

ISBN: 978-1-954396-93-7
Library of Congress Cataloging-in-Publication Data
Fever Road / Brawley

Printed in U.S.A.

Contents

Chapter One 1
Chapter Two 9
Chapter Three 25
Chapter Four 37
Chapter Five 44
Chapter Six 49
Chapter Seven 83
Chapter Eight 94
Chapter Nine 104
Chapter Ten 108
Chapter Eleven 125
Chapter Twelve 153
Chapter Thirteen 162
Chapter Fourteen 167
Chapter Fifteen 194
Chapter Sixteen 214
Chapter Seventeen 222
Chapter Eighteen 242
Chapter Nineteen 254

Chapter One

*If an ass goes traveling
He'll not come back a horse.*
Thomas Fuller, 1732

Now, when I try to conjure my essence as a young man, I see myself walking off my job at San Quentin Prison one night in 1962 and hitchhiking out to the Golden Gate Bridge with $37.00 in my wallet. I swung my backpack down by the southbound on-ramp, faced the traffic, and held up a big hand-lettered sign in my hands:

"AROUND THE WORLD
BACKWARDS"

"Around the world, huh?" said the carpenter in a pick-up truck who first gave me a ride. "And backwards yet! How long you been at it, son?"

"Just started this minute," I replied, then laughed to see the incredulous expression on his face. And I kept on laughing, it seems to me now, all the way to the Mexican border.

Raised on the grounds of state prisons, where my father was a Correctional Officer, then working as a guard on death row and the gun towers for over a year, I felt a bit like an escaped prisoner.

Later, I thought of this period in my life as Fever Road, or *Febris Viatica* in the more poetic Latin, as if it were some incurable disease of the road.

Yet, as time went by, I discovered that my syndrome was even more complex than I had originally supposed. Within its parameters there existed infinite species and subspecies. Several different varieties of the fever could attack the immune system simultaneously, their effects erratic and unpredictable in severity and duration. One type could rapidly metamorphose into another. Previously unknown biotypes could appear out of nowhere and disappear overnight or appear in alternate forms on alternate days. And the patient never acquired immunity, no matter how many times he might become infected.

My journey would take another seven years, though I intend no comparison to a certain ancient Greek, or to his modern resurrection by an Irish master. Still, seven years is a long time to travel the world alone. . . .

All right; I admit it. Although I'm an affable sort, my barroom camaraderie is rarely more than a shallow bit of farce. Truth is, I am often uneasy around people, especially if they insist on deep, soulful discussions. I have few close friends. When I move to a new place, I make lots of casual acquaintances but never get to know them except at the most superficial level. This suits me fine. Even when I am with the closest members of my family, I get shifty-eyed after an hour and make excuses to be off. As one of my ex-girlfriends says, I have "intimacy issues." In other words, I don't mind being on my own most of the time: When I was a young man, I recall, every time I found myself alone in another great foreign city, with my pockets empty, my stomach growling, it was like being born all over again.

As the years of my journey rolled by, I became more obsessive, inventing endless excuses to keep going. Eventually, I reached a point where I wanted neither the reality of my journey, nor its dramatic recreation in the journals I kept, to ever end. I had dozens of strange and desperate adventures, far too many to recount in these pages. Some were so implausible that if they had not happened to me, I would not have believed them myself. There were so many that when I try to summon them now, they flit by my consciousness in a fevered, dreamlike rush of color, movement, and sound. Like the times when:

A truck driver careening along a narrow, twisting dirt road, seven thousand vertical feet above an automotive graveyard in the Peruvian Andes, turned to reassure me that he still had three of his four wheels on the road. . . .

An Aymara Indian girl gave birth squatting on an open flat car, cut the umbilical cord herself, handed her wailing, dripping newborn to a friend, wiped the placenta up with a burlap sack, tossed it onto the railroad tracks, then calmly watched it recede into a tiny splotch of abstract crimson on the vast gray canvas of the Bolivian Altiplano. . . .

A cop in the Brazilian *Matto Grosso* arrested me and accused me of not being a "proper gentleman" for insufficiently tipping the middle-aged prostitute I had just used in a dirt-floored, cane-roofed shack beside an open sewer....

My ship ran into a hurricane with such mountainous seas that at one point I peered up through my twin portholes, as if through the eyes of a whale, to contemplate the frothing white surface of the South Atlantic Ocean far above me....

A Moroccan postal driver waved a pistol in my face, assuring me in bad French that if I was a "kike" and not the Christian I claimed to be, he would shoot me on the spot, dump my body in the desert, and nobody would be the wiser....

I ran with the bulls through the streets of Pamplona and made it into the bullring without a hitch, only to be smacked by the horns of a *toro* at the last minute. Thrown into the air, I could hear the spectators crying out in concern for my fate, *"Cuidado, hombre!"* Yet, I hit the ground and rolled to my feet without a scratch, then bowed to the adoring crowd. *"Bravo, gringo, bravo!"*

My haughty, Spanish girlfriend, inflamed by hours of flamenco and bottles of *Veterano,* leapt to the tabletop, kicked off all the glasses, then did a *zapateo* dance of such fire and *pasíon* that she filled our humid little gypsy cave with the sweet scent of her steaming underwear....

An old French conductor caught me red-handed with a forged Eurail Pass, but just laughed and said, "I'll let you go this time, young man, because Americans are usually such *bons clients*...."

I walked into a hospital in Geneva to sell blood. They took it from me standing up. I fainted from hunger, spraying red all over the room. Yet, when I tried to collect my money, they said, "*Desolé, monsieur*, but you're only paid according to what you deliver...."

Apprehended in a phony luggage insurance swindle in Bucharest, I was thrown into jail and subjected to a month of bread, water, and daily "Socialist Re-Education" sessions in Romanian....

My hitchhiking mate, Eve, and I were chased from an Eden-like apple orchard by an armed old Bulgarian Communist guard with the angry, bearded face of God....

A truck driver in Türkiye ran his hand up Eve's smooth white leg while his co-driver worked on my hairy one; then, thwarted in their ambitions, they switched, hoping for better luck next time....

A friendly, well-dressed young man in a brand-new Volkswagen Beetle pulled up and shouted, "Headed for Baghdad, guys?" in perfect California English, then left us in the middle of the bandit-infested Syrian Desert, with night coming on and jackals already howling when we refused to pay his outrageous fare....

A tiny, twisted, beggar boy in Benares, India, threw my proffered rupee back in my face with an irate: "But sir, this is quite inadequate to my needs...."

I sailed up the Saigon River on the good French ship *Cambodge* with Viet Cong on one side and South Vietnamese government troops on the other, lobbing mortars at each other over our heads....

I sat in the lotus position outside the Ryoanji Temple and Rock Garden for eight hours, collecting alms from the smiling, bowing, incredibly generous people of Kyoto, Japan, under a prayer flag and a sign that said, "*I have crossed the steaming Amazon, the burning Sahara, the frozen Hindu Kush. Won't you help me on my way*—"

I rode across the entire length of the Soviet Union on the Trans-Siberian Railway, from Vladivostok to the Finnish border, but saw nothing of the country because I was kept blind drunk by a reassigned platoon of loutish, bullying, Red Army soldiers.

"You drink vodka?"

"No thanks."

"You drink vodka!"

"I'm sorry, but—"

"YOU DRINK VODKA!"

"Okay, okay."

I got so cold one night in Bergen, Norway, that I kicked in the window of a liquor store just to be arrested and locked in a heated cell. . . .

I stepped onto Pier 6 in New York, after years on the road, and immediately got mugged by a great, scowling, Hulk Hogan look-alike who pistol-whipped me when I wasn't quick enough, laughed at the pathetic contents of my wallet, yet did not disdain to leave me penniless, and still three thousand miles from home. . . .

Yet, incredible though it may seem, given what I have recounted so far, my *tour du monde* could be quite humdrum for months at a time. Along the way (aside from various frauds, thefts, and smuggling attempts, which I only resorted to when hungry), I was gainfully employed in several legitimate or semi-legitimate capacities. I was, for instance, a truck driver for an American Catholic charity in Bolivia, and a copywriter/translator for the English language *Buenos Aires Herald* in Argentina. I was a bartender in Spain, a hop-picker in Kent, a Berlitz teacher in Paris, a street-sweeper in Amsterdam, and a dishwasher in Vienna. I was a moneychanger in Mumbai, a contraband watch salesman in Kathmandu, a movie extra in Tokyo, and a work-your-way deck hand on all the large stretches of water I had to cross.

The most rewarding part of the experience was that I had a girl in virtually every port, the only exception being Islamic countries—"If you look, you die," a Jordanian man once murmured, when he caught me gazing longingly at a minivan load of schoolgirls, "and if you touch, you double die...."

There were so many girls because in the Third World I really was—as a San Blas Indian woman once said when she caught sight of me plodding by her thatch-roofed village in the Darien Gap of Panama—"*Bonito!*"

I was handsome, charming, and supremely appealing to women simply because I happened to be of the conquering race, my nose was straight, I had all my teeth and hair, no pimples or smallpox scars, my clothes were decently made, and I had a college education. These things were extraordinarily rare in most of the world, I discovered; and it was even rarer that I could dance well, had a talent for mime and mimicry, could sing folk songs in a steady voice, and be witty and charming in the several languages I picked up along the way.

Even in a sophisticated city like Buenos Aires, the fact that I had hitchhiked from California to the southern tip of South America just for fun, not to work or visit relatives, was quite beyond their ken. They found me to be virtually superhuman.

In brief, I had never felt so attractive in my life, and though I certainly courted danger on my travels, I recall my amorous adventures far more vividly than all the others.

In this, I follow in a direct line from my ancestors.

Chapter Two

With him for a sire and her for a dam.
What should I be but just what I am?
EDNA ST. VINCENT MILLAY, 1920

This is no joke. I can prove it. Extensive genealogical research and abundant anecdotal evidence point to the fact that down through the generations, with few exceptions, the members of my family have been afflicted with a fatal combination of peculiarly aromatic pheromones, unusual quantities of dopamine, and in consequence grossly inflated libidos.

This is not to excuse our perennial peccadilloes, for our maker has granted us all free will, but we have indeed faced temptations far beyond those of most mortals.

Compounding our predisposition to stray, we are cursed with an unrestrained spirit of adventure, and a seeming indifference to risk that lasts far into old age. This, in turn, has led us far beyond the perils of the bedroom into impulsive journeys and flights from mundane reality, which have often ended in disaster: Among the first to quit the Old World, we were always first on the frontier, and thus first to be scalped by the indigenous natives.

To make things even worse, we seem to have acquired a constitutional inability to be happy with our own lot. To put it another way, we always want what the other guy's got, be it animate, inanimate, material, or immaterial. Which explains our astonishing upward and downward mobility over the past three or four centuries.

The syndrome, taken in its entirety and with its endless variations, is what my family has suffered over the generations, to the extent that somewhere along the line we produced an affectionate, humorous sobriquet: the 'Fever.' On my Mexican side, I've heard it referred to as *la fiebre*. And some humorous cleric back in Northern Ireland once dubbed it *febris familiaris*.

Whatever you want to call it, it has been and continues to be recognized by all of us as an indisputable part of our family heritage. Had we been sufficiently literate, we might well have extended the conceit and retained as our motto the immortal words of my esteemed master, James Joyce, and his wandering Irish Jew of an alter ego: "*Love, lie and be handsome, for tomorrow we die.*"

As a case in point, let me offer the example of my paternal great-grandmother, Letitia Jane Watkins. The attractive, well-bred daughter of an influential rancher, Civil War hero, and territorial legislator from the Tonto Basin of Arizona, Letitia was stricken with the 'Fever' at the very flowering of her maidenhood.

Defying not only family and friends, but also contemporary laws against "cohabitation," she absconded in the year 1889 with an infamously amoral gunslinger named Milt Brawley.

Letitia, whom I recall as a plump, sweet-natured old dowager who used to carve off the lean part of her meat to eat only the fat, rode with her criminal consort for five years, all over the Southwest, sleeping rough, stealing horses, rustling cattle, and dodging posses.

"Through thick and thin," she stuck with him, according to family lore, even though he cheated on her, gambled away all their money, risked death in street fights and pistol duels, and beat her so badly the one time she tried to complain that she miscarried their baby boy. She stuck with him, in fact, until he killed a man in a barroom brawl in Apache Junction and got locked away in Yuma Territorial Prison for the next ten years.

Forgive me if I now digress, but this is a telling, if self-damning detail: I recently acquired a grainy copy of the outlaw's old mugshot from the archives of the State of Arizona, and the son-of-a-bitch looks just like me.

Anyway, Letitia recovered from her common-law husband's abuse (once he was safely incarcerated). And with the characteristic resilience of our race, she married a cattleman from Red Rock, Arizona, in the year 1897. Upon his death in a riding accident the following year, she inherited his ranch and married again. In fact, she married five more times before her death, trading up each time, and widowed each time, until at the age of eighty-one she married a retired member of the Los Angeles city council.

Letitia had a daughter by the outlaw named Florence Emily Brawley, and the apple truly did not fall far from the tree. Pampered, willful, sweet sixteen, and living on the remote family ranch, she found herself in the year 1914 bored with country life, impatient with her virginity, and an easy mark for the 'Fever.'

Casting about for some source of amusement, she fixed on her mother's tall, handsome, green-eyed Mexican foreman, Jesus Robles, despite or precisely because he was a married man of thirty-six, with children her own age, and rumored to be her mother's ex-lover. Luring him out to the horse stable and up to the hayloft with obtuse questions of an equestrian nature, she succumbed to his half-reluctant arousal with only the most symbolic pretense of resistance . . .

"Nooo, nooo," she moaned, lifting her soft, white derriere, wriggling her saucy hips, pointing her toes, and kicking her little feet to aid in the removal of her lacy white knickers.

Do I know this for sure? No, but I do know enough of our ancestors' libidinal appetites to imagine it with some degree of probable accuracy. And since Grandma Florence has been dead for forty years, she is certainly in no position to refute my assumption.

Whatever the particulars, it is an indisputable fact that Florence was pregnant within a month. Within two, she had defied her irate mother, not to mention Jesus' apoplectic wife, and run off with him to Tucson.

Seven months later, she gave birth to my father, Ernesto Robles.

Fourteen years later, having borne Jesus six healthy children, she met Adólfo Corrales, a younger, handsomer, dark-eyed Mexican who lived with his sister right next door on North Ferro Avenue, and was seized by the 'fever' for the second time in her life. After a torrid year-long affair that was the scandal of the *barrio*, she abandoned her family to the care of her mother, ran off with Adolfo to East L.A., and lived with him there on Marengo Street, just down the road from the Chiquita Banana packing plant where they were both employed until his death at seventy years old.

Thereupon, the newly widowed Florence packed her bags and flew back to Arizona where she quickly took up with a wealthy, sickly, old, tomato rancher from Cochise County and—much to the chagrin of his heirs—married him within the year. But that's another story.

On the other side of the family, my maternal grandfather, Charles Holmes Wasson, in a fit of pique over some now long-forgotten slight, stole a horse off his father's plantation in the year 1895 and rode it all the way from Winn Parish, Louisiana, to Durango, Mexico, before his nineteenth birthday.

Representing himself as a recent graduate of Louisiana Tech (and with superbly self-forged documents to prove it), he acquired a job with an American-owned mining operation as an apprentice hydraulic engineer, moved in with a young local girl of Yaqui derivation, and sired three children with her, all before he was twenty-five.

In the year 1906, after years in Mexico, Charles read of the great earthquake which had befallen San Francisco. Sensing opportunity for a man of his "engineering" skills, he vowed to his common law wife that he would be back within the year, settled her and their brood of little *mestizos* in a rented adobe house, promised a small monthly stipend, and lit out for the Golden Gate by way of Chihuahua, El Paso, Phoenix, and Los Angeles.

He never saw his Mexican family again, for he ran smack into the 'fever' in El Paso, Texas.

Ambling down Prospect Street one morning in brand new lace-up boots and a pinstripe suit fresh off the rack, he spied a blond, buxom, white woman wheeling a two-year-old child in a pram and was instantly captivated despite himself.

"Beggin' your pardon, ma'am," he said, doffing his derby hat. "I'm new in town and I do believe I lost my way."

Charmed by his gallantry, and his tones of the Deep South (she was a Daughter of the Confederacy herself, from Madison County, Arkansas), my maternal grandmother, Lula Ann Hawkins, responded with a little curtsy and offered to show him the way, since she happened to be going in that direction herself.

He contrived to meet her the next day, and it was not long before they were strolling down Prospect Street together every morning. During long daily respites on a shady bench in Caruso Park, he commiserated with her discontent—dull, dry, provincial West Texas, a trainman husband who was always out of town—while her tranquilized toddler dozed through the heat. One thing led to another and, in the inexorable progression that seems to come so naturally to my family, it was not a month before he talked her into running off with him alone to California, leaving her sister-in-law and husband to pick up the pieces.

In time, Charles and Lula had six children, the third of whom was my mother, Helen Bee Wasson.

The prettiest of the Wasson girls, a little coquette, Helen was her father's pet. As she was growing up in the twenties, her family did well in construction, but by the time she was fourteen, in 1934, the construction business had dried up in the Depression, and they had been reduced to living in two rooms of their big, old, Victorian house on Central Avenue in Chino, California, while renting out the remainder to boarders.

Right next door to the Wassons, in another tall, vast, old Victorian, was the Brawley Mortuary & Ambulance Service. It catered to the Hispanic community in Chino for two very sound demographic reasons: Hispanics outnumbered Anglos two to one, and their mortality rate was vastly higher.

Residing on the premises and presiding over the enterprise, which flourished even in the depths of the Depression for the simple fact that illness and death are rarely unemployed, was Letitia's ex-brother-in-law from Arizona—a short, fat, bald, and nearly sightless character named Tom Brawley. Putting his profits from others' misfortunes to work, Tom had bought up most of the homes and businesses on Central Avenue as they went bankrupt in the Depression. And by 1935, he owned the whole block between Third and Fourth Streets, with the notable exception of the Wasson place.

Tom was renowned in Chino not only for his bumbling myopia, and the cold rationality of his acquisitive nature, but also for something "quite shocking" and singular in our family history. Though married to a Mexican woman of aristocratic pretensions who had provided him with three grown daughters and twelve grandchildren, he indulged himself in an "unnatural" pastime, shameless, indefatigable "pederasty," which was the scandal of the town.

Like an Oriental pasha, he kept his wife in the big house and a harem of poor, illegal, Mexican, orphan boys in an old barn behind his ambulance garage, rotating them on a nightly basis. The harem, or "stable" as it was known in Chino, was ruled with an iron hand by Ignacio "Eunuco" Contreras, an effeminate Mission Indian man with the withered face of an ancient crone, and his three, vicious, mastiff dogs, *Ciego*, *Sordo* and *Mudo*, or Blind, Deaf and Dumb.

Paradoxically, perhaps, Tom was also renowned in the town for his extreme generosity, an almost proverbial munificence enjoyed not only by the Blindness Fund, the Burial Fund, and several Baptist and Catholic charities, but also by the local police force, whose palms he greased on a monthly basis, and by his whole extended circle of friends and family. Thus, when his ex-sister-in-law, Letitia, asked for his help in placing the motherless, Robles children, he brought them all out from Arizona at his own expense, settling them on the empty third floor of his Victorian.

And he never touched either of the Robles boys, through all the years they lived there, though they were both, from his point of view, eminently desirable. On the contrary, he treated them—especially the better looking of the two—like little princes, buying them anything their hearts desired, sparing no expense on their education.

In short, he was the mother they had lost.

Their sisters, on the other hand, he benignly neglected, and they had to defend themselves against the venomous animosity of Tom's thin, sour-faced wife, all on their own.

The eldest of these sisters was a slight, curly-haired brunette who had been Maribel Robles in Tucson but was now known as Mabel Brawley.

At the behest of her Grandma Letitia—"You'll never get anywhere as little greasers!"—Mabel and all her five siblings had changed their surname to that of their jailbird maternal Grandpa Brawley and left all vestiges of their Hispanic heritage behind in Arizona.

In the year 1936, Mabel's next-door neighbor and best friend was Helen Wasson, a former classmate at Chino High School who had dropped out to help support her struggling family. Helen now worked part-time as usher at the Chino Theater, and she had been able to get Mabel on the payroll as well.

When Mabel worked nights, her brother Freddy Brawley (it had been Alfredo Robles in Arizona) would pick her up in a big, old Packard, a Black Maria. Being the Latin gentleman that he was, he volunteered to give Helen a nightly lift as well. Tall, slender, and good-looking, with blue eyes, freckles, and the wavy, luxuriant, auburn hair of his mother and grandmother, Freddy had been a star athlete in high school, student body president at Pomona Junior College, and now made good money working for his Uncle Tom, learning the mortician's trade.

On their nightly trips from the movie house, Freddy and Helen chatted and flirted as if they could not get enough of each other, leaving Mabel to glower, ignored, in back. Within no time, it seemed, they were, as one said in Southern California at the time, "a very hot item."

Having retrieved the girls at the movie house and left his sulky sister off at the funeral parlor, Freddy would drive five miles out into the beet fields near Chino Prison then park between the dark and fecund furrows. There he would labor for hours without success to get Helen to lie with him on one of the empty coffins (which, rumor had it, Uncle Tom used repeatedly) in the rear section of the Black Maria.

"Now, don't git me wrong, Freddy," she would say, in the vestigial Southern accent of her family, "I ain't squeamish about death, but I do intend to stay a virgin 'till the day I walk down the aisle."

Accordingly, within the year, they were engaged to be married.

Then Freddy made a big mistake.

He decided to have a belated engagement party in the funeral parlor, to which he would invite all his friends and family. Despite misgivings, he asked his older brother Ernie Brawley (*né* Ernesto Robles) to come along as well, though they had forever been rivals.

Ernie did not get into town often. For the past few years, he had been working six days a week as a correctional officer at Chino Prison and living in bachelor quarters on the grounds. Before that, he was at Pomona Junior College, so he had not seen Helen since she was a little snippet of a thing. Yet, the instant he walked into the party, the music, the laughter, the joyful voices, the colorful costumes of friends and family, all faded into the remote background. The only thing he could see was Helen: her elegant aquiline features, her big, brown, heavily lidded eyes, her red, red lips.

He saw her from across the crowded funeral parlor as if across an empty stage. Surrounded by a gaggle of female friends in hats, veils, and bright afternoon attire, she stood out among them as if alone under a powerful spotlight. In a little straw hat with a ribbon at the back, a long, wraparound satin dress with ruffled shoulders, a big, black belt cinched tight to accentuate her tiny waist, pointed two-tone shoes with Cuban heels, she looked years beyond her age, the very image of thirties' chic.

Instantly, Ernie was smitten with the 'fever.'

Not the least part of his attraction, as I would deduce many years later, was the fact that she was his brother's girl.

To make things worse, it was fever at first sight for Helen as well, despite her vows to Freddy, despite the gravity of the setting, despite the fact—as she would never cease to lament for years to come—that Ernie possessed fewer of those attributes that normally set young girls' hearts atwitter.

Freddy was tall and slender, while Ernie was short and squat. Freddy had sharply chiseled features, pale skin, fine auburn hair, whereas Ernie's face was square, swarthy, nondescript, and his coarse black hair was quickly receding. Freddy was affable as an Irishman, but Ernie was dour as an Indian. Freddy had cultivated Uncle Tom, so he had bright prospects in the mortuary. Ernie, however, had forsaken Tom as a teenager, calling him "a fat, blind, prancing queen," so he had only the toil and danger of a low-paying prison job to anticipate.

Even myself, when older, wondered at my mother's inexplicable decision, until my Great-grandma Letitia, when I visited her in Pasadena shortly before her demise, set me straight.

"Love is blind," she said, "once the fever gets ahold of you."

Great-grandma didn't know anything about dopamine, pheromones, or libidos back in those days, but it all amounts to the same thing, doesn't it?

Yet, Helen's blindness turned out to be prescient in this case, for one evening, years later, facing prison for his third felony drunk-driving charge, Freddy shot himself in the bathtub while his fourth wife was downstairs in the mortuary kitchen preparing dinner.

But that was to come. In the present, Ernie and Helen had other things on their minds. Having established their mutual admiration by instantaneous eye contact on the night of her engagement party, they found it both exceedingly difficult and immensely frustrating to assuage their raging fever in the days that followed. This was because her fiancé was jealous-hearted, suspicious, and watched her like a hawk, while Ernie had only one day off a week.

"Where there's a will, there's a way," though, as Grandma Wasson used to say, so it wasn't long before they were meeting secretly, late at night, on the back seat of Ernie's Model "A" Ford, in the alleyway behind the Wasson place. And this time, Helen made no protests about her virginity. Or, as my master,

James Joyce, had put it, more poetically: "*undoing with sweet pudor her belt of rushrope, offered her allmoist yoni.*"

Chino was a small community, its white population in those days positively minuscule. Very soon, all the Anglos in town, with one exception, knew exactly what was up.

Freddy could not figure out why everyone was tittering behind his back until one night, driven by a perfectly reasonable suspicion, he crept around behind the Wasson place and caught them in the act.

Then came a yowling of such ferocity and profanity that it woke the entire neighborhood, followed by a flurry of female finery being rapidly set straight, then a male shouting match punctuated by much shoving and cursing. Helen ran into the house crying, and the argument ended in fisticuffs, with Ernie the loser. Freddy stomped off, and Ernie lay bleeding, half-conscious, in the alleyway, until Grandpa Wasson's cocker spaniel licked him awake.

The brothers never spoke another word 'till the day they died. Word of the scandal got around fast. Soon Ernie and Helen found themselves to be outcasts in the town, scorned by even family and friends. To make things worse, Helen missed her next two periods. The Wasson family found this less troublesome than the fact that the putative father, Ernie, unlike his brother, Freddy, was a throwback to his Mexican half. Or, as Grandma Wasson called him, "that damn little wetback-lookin' hombre."

The lovers decided to elope, but since Helen was only sixteen, unable to marry without parental consent, she had to find someone to stand up for her. Yet, everyone she asked turned her down flat. Finally, in desperation, she convinced Ernie to phone his estranged mother in East L.A.

"At least, with her record, she's no one to cast stones," Helen said, and she was right.

Without any fuss at all, Grandma Florence took a day off from her job at the Chiquita Banana plant, accompanied them in Ernie's rattling Model "A" Ford to Tijuana, Mexico, and signed as a witness in the quickie chapel where they wed.

There was no honeymoon, of course, for there was no money for such things in those days, and Ernie had to get back to work at the prison.

The Sunday after the wedding, however, in a move that Helen would always extol as the epitome of their romance, he drove her up to Puddingstone Reservoir, in the foothills of the San Gabriel Mountains, and feted her with a picnic of ham and cheese sandwiches with fizzy pink California champagne.

How do I know this?

Because eight years later, in 1944, when my father was in the US Army, Mama drove me and my little sisters up to Puddingstone on a Sunday picnic excursion. There was a misty, faraway look in her eyes as she sat under the gnarly oak trees, gazing down the hillside over waves of yellow, wild oats and orange, California poppies to the shimmering blue lake, recounting her tale of romance to us. Yet there was another, deeper glint there as well. I did not understand it at the time, but I found it so singularly interesting that I committed it to memory.

Only years later did I finally understand what the look in my mother's eyes meant:

They had made love there, under the oak trees, on the yellow hill above the lake.

Another of the serious flaws in my family's bloodline, one that I have neglected so far to admit, is that we are without exception tellers of tall tales (or "congenital liars," as one of my ex-girlfriends would have it). Early in my life, therefore, I concocted a version of events that placed the moment of my conception not in a dark alleyway, in the backseat of a Model "A" Ford, but on a sunny hill above Puddingstone Reservoir.

And I have maintained that version to this very day. But it stops right here.

For this is to be my day of reckoning.

There was, however, one real moment of love in my parents' lives that I personally witnessed and will always remember with warmth and affection.

It happened like this. My father was being shipped out from Fort MacArthur in San Pedro, California, to Fort Bliss, Texas. Before he left, he phoned my mother. He told her to drive to Pomona at a specific time, wait by the station, and wave at him as his army train went by. So, my mother packed me and my little sisters, Diane and Lenor, into our Pontiac, along with our Grandma Florence, and did just as my father had suggested. As his train went by, he leaned out and waved to us, and we all laughed, shouted our love to him, and waved back.

But he was gone in a flash, which did not suit Mother Helen at all. She threw the Pontiac into gear and raced off after the train, running red lights and driving at high speed 'till it pulled over in the countryside to let another train pass. My mother drove off the highway and made it halfway across a wet field, only stopping when her car got stuck in the mud. But that didn't stop her. She leapt out and raced across the field toward the train, while all the soldiers cheered her on. She ran up to my father's window, jumped high into his arms, legs dangling, and they kissed long and passionately, as the entire trainload of soldiers shouted in delight. While we were all transfixed by this vision, Grandma Florence turned to us and said, "You wanna know what love is, kids? That is what love is!"

And none of us ever forgot it.

Chapter Three

Being young is greatly overestimated.
Mary Quant, 1934

My mother was delighted when I was born, by all accounts. Not only was I large and healthy, but I looked nothing like Freddy, which she hoped would put to rest all rumors of who the true daddy might be. To remind her neighbors in Chino, should they forget, she called me "Ernie Junior."

My first memory is of a face. A young, pretty woman with shiny, bobbed, black hair, big brown eyes, and a gently curving nose, was bending over me, smiling. This was my mommy's face, I knew. And it filled me with a sense of shivery happiness and well-being.

Thirty-one years later, I would marry that face, or a reasonable facsimile thereof.

My second memory is of a face as well. I was playing with my daddy on the grass in my maternal grandparents' backyard on Central Avenue. My daddy disappeared and a dark, round visage appeared above me. He had big, pointed ears, a thatch of black hair, bright white teeth, and his smile was not pleasant at all.

He was one of Tom Brawley's orphan boys, his favorite, the only one he let lead him around like a blind dog. I knew him. His name was Tito, but everyone called him "*Retoñito*" or "Squirt" because of his stunted growth.

"*Ven, ven, vente conmigo,*" he whispered urgently, "come, come, come with me."

Grasping my hand, he pulled me into his arms. Then he ran with me across the yard, out the back gate, down the alley, into the rear gate of Tom's place, and through the squeaky door of the tool shed, even though I bellowed my guts out all the way.

"No, no! Lemme go, lemme go!"

Inside the shed, an immensely bright shaft of light streamed down through a crack in the wooden shingles, illuminating spider webs, old, broken tools, and a greasy workbench. The place smelled of must, oily sand, and pigeon shit.

Still smiling, Tito laid me out on the workbench, shaking his head, putting a finger to his lips when I kicked my feet and screamed, "I want my mommy!"

Into the pocket of his tan corduroy pants, he slid a hand (a clean, long-fingered hand that smelled of red peppers) and out came a small gleaming knife.

Looking up at him, eyes popping, I saw the smile fade from Tito's face. Quick as a snake, he reached down with his other hand to clutch me by the throat. "*No te mueves,* don't move," he hissed, and cut through the front of my bibbed, cotton shorts with one long slice of the blade.

Then he was doing something to me with the knife, something that hurt more than anything, something that made me shriek in terror, something that would wake me up screaming for the rest of my life.

"*Voy hacerte una chamacita como yo,*" he whispered, in his slow, singsong *Norteno* accent, ignoring my cries, looking me straight in the eyes. "I'm gonna make you a little girl like me."

My body went into spasms. My heart seemed to burst from my chest. Just as everything started to go black, my grandma, Lula Ann, burst through the door, slamming it open with a big bang, causing the dust and light to swirl about in a celestial, slow-motion cloud.

Grey hair flying, eyes big as eggs, mouth wide open, howling like a banshee, she grabbed a broken broomstick from beside the door, whirled on the cowering, whimpering Tito, beat him into a cobwebby corner, and started jabbing at him with the sharp end of the broomstick, right in the face, right in the eye, right in the ass.

My mother ran in behind her, crowding the tiny space with hysteria: "Oh my god, my god, my god! Your dad was supposed to be watching you! Where's he at? Where's he at?"

Scooping me up in her arms, she raced across the littered yard, up the back steps of the mortuary and through the screen door. She ran through the kitchen, ignoring Zita, Mabel, Letitia, Fred, and the others gathered at the table over lunch, then flung open the door to Tom Brawley's office.

Seated corpulently at his desk in a black mourning suit and a green visor cap, under an adjustable reading lamp, the undertaker was bent over a stack of bills and receipts, perusing them from an inch away with his magnifying glass. An empty lunch tray lay beside him on the floor.

"Look! Look at this, you blind-ass faggot!" my mother shrieked, kicking the lunch tray out of the way, sending dishes clattering against the wall.

Then, thrusting me out over his desk, right up into his face, turning me this way and that, flinging blood all over his white shirt and the papers before him, she wailed as if the earth had split open and all the heavens had fallen, "LOOK! LOOK WHAT ONE OF YOUR DAMN LITTLE ORPHAN BOYS HAS DONE!"

"Where the hell is Ignacio?" Tom demanded indignantly, spinning nimbly around in his swivel chair to face her without a trace of remorse. "He's supposed to be watchin' over them boys."

The next thing I knew, we were in one of Tom's ambulances with the siren wailing. Uncle Freddy was driving. We pulled up in front of Pomona General Hospital. A nurse carried me into an operating room. Then something happened to me that I rapidly contrived to forget, to grow scar tissue over. . . .

Cut.

Segue to a bathtub a year or two later. "Mommy, what is this scar on me down here?"

"Why, honey, that's the seam where God sewed you together when he made you."

"And why do I have three eggs down here?" I asked. "One big one and two small ones, not two the same size, like the other boys."

"Because, my dearest, God loved you so much that he wanted to give you a little something extra," she said.

And I chose to believe her.

Yet, in my heart, and lower down, I always knew.

The kid, Tito Retoñito, disappeared, along with the orphan boys' straw boss, Ignacio *"Eunuco"* Contreras, but I never heard of any formal accusation or prosecution for the crime.

My family always suspected that Tom's wife, Zita, put Tito up to it, after sending Ignacio off on an errand, to get back at Tom. Though there was not a shred of evidence for this, none of us ever spoke to her again.

Later, I learned that my father had gone off for a quickie with his "floozy," thinking I would be safe in my grandparents' backyard. My mother never forgave him for it; and he never forgave me for destroying his marital bliss, for wordlessly reminding him of his guilt. Our relations, therefore, were distant and formal all through his life.

Except when it came to corporal punishment.

Then it got personal.

As for Tom, he rapidly hushed the whole thing up with generous grants to the police department, the district attorney, and to my mother, too, when she threatened to sue him.

Not that he intended to give up on his orphan boys.

When I was twelve years old, in Mr. Fox's sixth grade class at Chino Elementary School, one of my classmates was a spectacularly good-looking kid named Narciso Calderon.

Due to repeated disciplinary problems, Narciso was now in his third year of sixth grade. At fourteen, he was far too old to be hanging about with us, but he seemed far too young for the shiny, Ford V8 convertible that he drove to school every day.

When I asked the how and why of it, he brusquely replied, as if the answer were self-evident, "I'm one of Tom Brawley's boys."

It was also in the sixth grade that I had to address the issue of my birth for the first time. Out on the playground after lunch, a bunch of us boys were talking about this and that when the subject of birthdays and anniversaries came up. In the ensuing discussion, I innocently divulged the information that my parents' wedding anniversary was in late March, and my birth date was in early October of the same year.

"But that ain't right, Ernie!" they all shouted, laughing, and pointing at me. "That ain't right!"

"What do you mean it ain't right?

"*Que carajo!*" Narciso exclaimed. "You're not supposed to be born seven months after your folks was married! Supposed to be born *nine* months after, you dumb shit!"

"You don't even know what you're talkin' about," I said. But that evening when I got home, I went straight to my mother, demanding an explanation.

"Now, you listen to me, boy, that is a damn lie. You go tell them boys that you were a 'preemie.'"

"What's a 'preemie,' Mom?"

"God brought you into the world two months early."

"But you were always bragging about how big I was when I was born, Mom. Eight pounds, you said."

I date my first instant of adulthood from that precise moment, for when I saw the flesh of my mother's face and neck go red with embarrassment, and a kind of anxious, cornered look appear on her face, my heart went out to her in pity and affection, so I quickly added, "uh... you're right, Mom. I see what you mean. I'm gonna go tell them boys they're cuckoo!"

It was only a few weeks after that epiphany, perhaps not by chance, when I had the first of those feverish experiences that would one day rule my life, as they had ruled the lives of my ancestors.

At the desk beside mine in Mr. Fox's class sat a dark and beautiful Basque girl with the most delectable budding breasts. Her name was Suzanne Mutaberria. All through the early weeks of the school year, she kept glancing across at me out of the corner of her big, black, heavy-lashed eyes. Yet only then did I begin to consider the full significance of those glances. Only then did my little heart start to go pitter-patter, pitter-patter.

Though Suzanne and I eventually reached a kind of silent meeting of the minds, we were far too shy to declare our feelings for each other. Luckily, there was one place, outside of school, where we always found ourselves together: the Saturday matinee at the New Chino Theater....

I began my campaign by sitting alone a few seats behind her and her little sister, Julie. Then, over time, encouraged by Suzanne's meaningful backward glances, I wended my way closer until I was right behind her, then two seats down from her. Finally, I was sitting right next to her, the rare recipient of fleeting glimpses from her bewitchingly dark eyes. We never said a word to each other, but slowly, slowly, over all the long weeks of winter, I worked my arm around her soft little shoulders until, holding my breath, heart stopped, I was touching the tender, yielding flesh of her upper arm. By spring, I knew the exquisite pleasure of holding her small warm hand in mine. Her little sister, Julie, enthralled by the cartoon, the serial, the double features, seemed to notice nothing. Yet, when late that spring I stole a kiss—a kiss I can still feel, still taste—little Julie went straight home to her mom, who instantly put a stop to it.

For weeks after that, I suffered in fretful, fevered silence, alone at every Saturday matinee, until I could take it no more.

I got an after-school job delivering the evening edition of the *Pomona Progress-Bulletin* simply because the route went by Suzanne's house on Riverside Drive.

Day after day, I rode by very slowly, hoping that I might see her, only to spend the rest of my long route smarting from disappointment. Then one afternoon, I did see her! She was standing on the lawn out front, behind a white picket fence, watering her mother's flowers. And even now, seventy-five years later, when Suzanne is probably someone's grey-haired great-granny, the vision of her standing on the wet grass in her bare tanned feet, still—as the songsters of our era had it—"makes my heart skip a beat."

Barefoot, wearing white shorts and a pink, sleeveless blouse, her long, dark legs glistened in the California sunshine. She had pinned up her thick, black hair, yet strands curled about her ears. Smiling about something, but not about me, she had not even caught sight of me yet.

Entranced by the vision, I started pedaling toward her across Riverside Drive, a major thoroughfare, without thinking. Directly behind me a horn honked, and brakes screeched. Startled, I was about to turn to confront the obvious but chose to risk another peek at Suzanne.

She had heard. She had seen me. She was pointing behind me in alarm. Eyes wide, mouth hanging open, she screamed at me, but I heard nothing. In a delirium of joy at this evidence of her concern and affection, I turned to confront my coming death with perfect equanimity.

It only took an instant, but I recall it perfectly. A big, black, Buick Roadmaster was skidding sideways at me in slow motion, in absolute silence, though I could see its fat-faced driver grimacing, fighting the wheel.

I tried to pedal out of his way, but it was only an instinctive reflex.

There was no dream of escape.

Then the sound switched back on. I could hear the tires screeching across the asphalt, and Suzanne's reedy little voice somewhere far off in the distance, screaming my name at the top of her lungs.

"Ernie!"

Wham! The Buick hit me, but my bike took the brunt of the blow and flew off into the irrigation ditch on the other side of the road.

I never lost consciousness. Smacking into the blacktop, I skidded across its rough, gravelly surface on my hands, elbows, knees, and toes, grating them all to the bone.

The driver rushed up, started hollering down at me.

"You all right? Why the hell did you cut in front of me like that, kid?"

Yet, all I was looking for was Suzanne. If she would just come and sit down beside me, cradle my head in her lap, run her cool hands over my burning face, croon to me like a baby, it would be worth it all. . . .

Unfortunately, that is only the stuff of fairy tales. In fact, Suzanne's mother ran out of the house, dragged her back inside, and phoned the police. A few minutes later, an ambulance screeched up and hauled me away.

I was laid up for two weeks, in terrible pain; yet, incredibly, no bones were broken.

I received no get-well card from Suzanne, no phone call enquiring about my health, though I waited for one every day.

That autumn, when school started, she was nowhere to be found.

Later, I heard that she had been sent to Catholic school.

In November of that same eventful year, my mom caught my dad fucking around with a rich widow from Claremont and kicked him out of the house. Why she picked this one instance, when he'd been doing it from year one with every available woman within thirty miles, is any body's guess.

She took to drink about that time, blaming it on my dad, though it ran in her family, along with their many other defects. She was mentally absent much of the time from then on, every day from about noon until midnight, and there were times when I had to care for her like a baby.

"I was the father of my mother," I wrote in my journal once, exaggerating, as is my wont.

But she never let us go hungry or kept a dirty house. And my siblings Diane, Lenor, and Douglas turned out all right (I count myself as the exception) despite the cursed genes that we bear, so I don't begrudge her tippling.

What I do begrudge is this: No matter how befuddled my mother got, she rarely slept alone, and some of the trash that she brought home . . . whew! Especially the ones she met in her brief flings with Alcoholics Anonymous. She never gave up on them either, not at least until she was to the point where she had to walk about her trailer house dragging an oxygen tank behind her. She died not of drink, as we had all expected, but of the lung cancer that she contracted from smoking two packs of "ciggies" a day for sixty years.

My dad married the rich widow, who only got richer. Yet, he never stopped fucking around either, not at least until after his second heart attack, when he was close to eighty.

As for Suzanne Mutaberria, I ran into her once again when I was a sophomore in high school. . . . The occasion was a basketball game between Chino High and St. Francis Xavier. Suzanne was walking with a girlfriend down in front of the bleachers at halftime, dressed in a tight white sweater, blue pedal pushers, and black shoes with French heels. Prettier than ever, all grown up now, with a confident air, a womanly voice, she laughed at what her friend was saying as if the entire gym were hers for the taking. I knew she'd caught a glimpse of me out of the corner of her eye, but I didn't have the nerve to run down and talk to her.

She did not seem inclined to pursue the point either.

Why should she, after all?

In tacky blue jeans and a flannel shirt that my mom got from a Sears & Roebuck catalogue, I was still just as skinny and undeveloped as a sixth grader, my voice afflicted with an adolescent squawk.

Time had stopped for me, it seemed, when I got smacked by a car outside her house on Riverside Drive, when I gave up everything for a glance. But for Suzanne, with her swaying hips, it was still in motion.

Chapter Four

"A boy's will is the wind's will."
Longfellow, 1858

When I was sixteen, I finally started to fill out, and I got a part-time job washing dishes at the roadside diner where my mom waited tables. So, at last, I could buy myself decent clothes.

That summer, too, I got my first car. I did not buy the car myself.

Truth is, it was a kind of bribe.

The way it happened... After my parents broke up, my Aunt Mabel's husband, Uncle Frank, used to come over and drink with my mom late at night, when we kids were supposed to be asleep. Then one night, I got up to pee and caught them *in flagrante delicto* on the living room rug. It was the most shocking vision of my life since by then neither of them was very pretty to look at. Nobody said anything at the time. We just gawked at each other for an instant, then I hastened from the room.

Yet, it was not a week later when my Uncle Frank came by with his nifty, little '49 Ford Sedan (a car I had already dubbed "The Jungle Cruiser" for its uncanny, Jeep-like, off-road capacities), and said, "I was all set to trade it in for a new one. But the little they wanted to give me for it, I thought, 'what the hell. Ernie needs a car.'"

Nothing more was said, but I got his meaning anyway.

Now I had me some wheels!

Hence, when I went back to high school that fall, I felt much better about myself.

My English teacher, Mr. Millhizer, liked my writing, so he offered me a weekly column in the school newspaper. Combining juvenile humor and veiled salacious gossip, it quickly became immensely popular.

I called it *"Ernie's Brawlesque."*

At this time also, I suddenly found myself quite sought after by the girls. One of those who came my way was Terri Lindstrom. Already a woman, fully developed at the age of fourteen, she would never change much from what she was then. Tall, slender, with ice-blue eyes, a thin prominent nose, full lips, the luminous Laplander skin, and white-blond hair of some Scandinavians, she might have been a model, had fate not other plans for her.

Hers was the gawky kind of sexiness that some tall girls possess; she was so excessively feminine that she could not run without flailing her arms and knocking her knees. Placid, sensible, but only average in the brain department, she was a born mother. Even as a young teenager, the signal she gave off was extreme fecundity, which could be a real turn-on.

Attractive though Terri might have been (Queen of the Sophomore Hop!), the basic docility of her nature precluded any thought of fever or desperation, which suited me fine. Ever since my experience with Suzanne, I had attempted to keep myself safely immunized against the contagion of my ancestors. What I needed, I told myself, was a nice, steady girl. Unrestrained passion—as nature, nurture and sad experience had taught me—led only to despair.

We met on a double date and went through the typical fifties' experience of dating, going steady, petting, heavy petting, and finally "going all the way." The last part came on New Years Eve, 1954, in a lovers' lane overlooking Los Serranos Lake. Still only fifteen and seventeen, and years before the institution of high school Sex Ed classes, we really had not a clue what we were doing. Incredible as it may seem now, we were not even sure where babies came out, the front or the back. . . .

I remember the whole thing as if it happened yesterday: Laying Terri down on the rough felt seat of the Jungle Cruiser, I smothered her lips with mine. Sucked her tongue 'till she started to pant and get hot to the touch. Jerked her sweater over her head. Removed her bra by the simple expedient of breaking the snap. Wrapped my mouth around a nipple and sucked till she screeched in pleasure. As she arched and kicked to help me, I slipped her panties over her curving hips and buttocks, her slender legs, and long-toed feet. Then I touched her where she wanted me to.

"Oooooooh," she moaned; I can hear her now. Her voice, deepened by desire, was no longer that of a young girl, but of a woman with immediate needs.

By then, the surprising wetness that my fingers had provoked, and its intoxicating smell, had inflamed me past enduring. Terri was drenched with longing, even into the wiry triangle of her pubic hair. I was bigger in my hand than I had ever imagined I could be.

Yet, when "the moment of truth" came as she cried, "Yes, Ernie, yes!" I just could not seem to find the right spot. The mysterious crevice I had discovered about her underbody was so incredibly long, with so many smooth, slick folds and orifices, that it seemed impossible to plumb.

"Help me!" I whispered frantically. "I don't know where to put it!" But Terri was far too shy, too "decent" a girl, to help.

It never occurred to me that I might simply grip her delectable inner thighs and spread her legs to make the job easier, so I just kept humping and jabbing here and there, like a dog at a bitch, until quite by chance I hit the jackpot. I plunged through those indescribably soft, slippery red ruffles and wimples—"*white thy fambles, red thy gan, and thy quarrons dainty is*" says the master—and into the hollow, sucking, life-giving maw that lay below.

Wave after wave of pleasure ran through me, a tingling and shuddering of such intensity that it beggared all else in my brief life.

Terri sobbed and moaned from somewhere deep inside, so deep that at one point it seemed her entire body was being invaded by some kind of incubus.

This takes a long time to describe, but it was over in a flash. Eight or ten thrusts and I shuddered, cried aloud, and spurted inside her in three great heaving gobs.

Ten minutes later, we were at it again, but this time I did not come so fast.

"Give me a baby!" Terri pleaded (this, too, pure animal instinct), as our lovemaking reached its third crescendo. "I don't care! I don't care!"

Afterwards, when we were sitting naked together in the back seat of the Jungle Cruiser, reliving our fantastic experience like the excited teenagers we were, Terri reached two long fingers down inside her still hot and humid organ, murmuring half to herself, "I wonder what..." and brought a dripping mass of our mingled juices to her nose.

"Ah!" she said, inhaling deeply into her lungs; and then, with a smile of such primordial female contentment that I can see it today, she proffered her sopping fingers to me and breathed these words wise beyond her years, "Smell, Ernie. It's the smell of life!"

Not only did I sniff them, but I sucked them dry, and I had never tasted anything so good.

"What about blood?" I asked. "Isn't there supposed to be blood?"

"Oh, I think I already broke it last year, on my bicycle crossbar," she said, which seemed perfectly plausible to me at the time.

It was a miracle that I did not get Terri Lindstrom pregnant. If I had, we might still be married today. We made love for two years, taking only the most rudimentary precautions, and she never missed a period. I even began to worry that the injury I had incurred as a child, in Tom Brawley's tool shed, had rendered me impotent.

Considering the sublime joys of our first experience, we quickly settled into the routine of a long-term relationship. Our lovemaking became a happy, satisfying, yet utterly normal experience. I recall a few special times in the beginning—once in the snow at Mount Baldy, once in the shallows of the Santa Ana River, once on Terri's living room rug while her mother pruned the rose tree just outside the window—but there were fewer novelties as time went on.

This, too, suited me fine.

Even our breakup came without climax. We just drifted apart when I was in college and Terri was still in high school, and it was over before we realized it. I must admit, it was a shock when I saw her "taking the drag" down Central Avenue with her new boyfriend, an ex-Marine named Dom Spatafore, but I soon got over it.

Six years later, I heard that Terri had married Dom. They moved to the Bay Area. He got a job in the Oakland Police Department and quickly rose to the position of detective sergeant. They had three kids and a home in the East Bay hills. Everything was going along fine, apparently, until one night, while off duty, Dom intervened in a neighborhood marital disturbance. The distraught husband pulled a gun, fired without warning, and hit Dom in the lower spine, paralyzing him for life. A year or two later, despondent over his condition and drinking heavily, he left Terri, I heard, to "set her free," and committed suicide with his service revolver not long afterwards.

That was the last I ever heard of Terri, but I still think of her with the greatest sympathy and respect. And I often wonder why such a sweet, wholesome, All-American girl was dealt such a lousy hand in life, when bastards like her ex-boyfriend, who later became known as "Dirty Ernie," are sitting relatively pretty.

Chapter Five

O! Many a shaft, at random sent
Finds mark the archer little meant!
Sir Walter Scott, 1815

My life as an undergraduate—six years of night classes at San Francisco State College while commuting to eight-hour day jobs at the Southern Pacific Railroad and then as a guard at San Quentin Prison—was lengthy, arduous, and enlivened by few surprises or successes.

All through college, I sought out sweet-natured, unadventurous girls, like Terri Lindstrom, who displayed no signs of my family's cursed fever. What I craved in a woman most, I thought, was not a wild and exciting nature, but a stable, compliant one. The problem was that girls of that description rarely held my attention for long.

The quintessential example being Helga Hackenbroich, a sprightly, artless, red-cheeked, Bavarian peasant girl I met in

Das Blaue Engle, the *gemutlich* German restaurant where she worked in the Richmond District.

After dining there for several weeks (it was conveniently located on Park Presidio Boulevard, just off my daily route from San Francisco State to San Quentin Prison), I chatted her up one night and managed to get her phone number. On my next day off, I asked her out for a drive.

On a warm, sunny, California day in early November, we drove up to Stinson Beach, piled out of my car, and ran down to the water. I stripped to my skivvies, dove in, and went for a swim, though the water was like ice. Helga rolled up her Capri pants and danced in the foam, kicking spray. Young and vibrant, only nineteen, her blond curls and rosy cheeks shone in the sun.

Later, we went for a walk in the sand, and Helga matched me stride for stride, though she was slight. Every time she saw a loose dog, she chased after it, grabbed it by the chops, leaned down, and spoke German to it very seriously, as if to a rowdy child.

"Bist du ein gut hund, mein freund, oder nicht?" she asked, in the biblical-sounding German familiar. "Beist thou not a good hound, my friend, or not?"

We lingered on the beach all day, sipping red wine from a jug, watching the sun go down into the sea. In the chill, salty, twilight, I opened her blouse, pushed her back in the sand, and kissed her small white breasts, her tiny pink nipples.

On our way home on the Coast Highway, she left her bra off under her blouse. Whenever we hit a rough spot in the road, Helga bounced on the seat, but her breasts did not even jiggle. And when she leaned against me to kiss my ear, I felt their firm, young, nakedness against my bare arm.

I stayed over at her apartment that night.

And so, it began.

We liked each other well enough, and we got along all right, but it quickly became evident that our disparities in language, intelligence, education, and general culture were insurmountable.

We went out for a year and broke up, by mutual consent. A month later, she found herself pregnant. I readily admitted to being the father of the child and even provided her with a small monthly allotment from my correctional officer's salary. After all, her pregnancy was living proof that my grievous childhood wound had left me scarred but not unmanned.

Out of fear, desperation, and habit, Helga clung to me till the end. I understood her religious scruples against aborting the child, and saw her (indifferently, I admit) through her pregnancy. I was there for the birth and supported her decision to give the child up for adoption.

Finishing off my last few credits at San Francisco State, working double shifts at San Quentin, I prepared to set off on a long-planned hitchhike around the world. I dealt with Helga's growing tendency to cling by promising to write faithfully and keep sending her monthly checks until she was back on her feet. This, to be frank, was a promise I had no intention of keeping.

Five months later, when I was in Guayaquil, Ecuador, sponging off some Peace Corps members who had a big house near the beach, I learned that Helga had returned to her family in Germany.

Three years later, when I was living in Paris, teaching ESL at the *Pantheon-Sorbonne*, Helga wrote me a letter asking if she could come and visit me for a few days. Reluctantly, I agreed on the condition that we not sleep together, a condition I instantly revoked on her first night in town.

Yet, just as I feared, our renewed relations were not a success. Though she had the tact, and the good sense not to mention my unpaid debt, she did start to cling and get sentimental again.

"*Bist du nicht der Vater von mein Sohne*? Beist thou not the Father of mine Son?" she asked. "How could I not feel this way?"

Within a day or two (and without any overt pushiness at all), Helga was like an albatross around my neck. As a direct consequence of which, one night in *La Palette*—a Left Bank bistro full of my friends—I found myself making a joke at her expense. Deeply offended, she left the table in tears, refusing all my apologies.

She departed for Munich the next day, and I never heard from her again.

The weird thing is, I cannot, to this day, recall what I said that insulted her so.

I do remember one thing, though.

After Helga left the table, one of my closest friends in Paris, a French painter named Bill Pestre, said, "*Tu sais, mon vieux, tu n'aimes pas les gents; tu les baises.* You know, man, you don't love people; you fuck them."

It hit home, what Bill said. And even now, when he has rested with his ancestors in the *Cimetière de Montparnasse* for fifteen years, it still smarts, precisely because there may be a smidgeon of truth in it.

To counter those terrible, biting words, I am tempted now to just cry out into the darkness and emptiness of time and space, "I'm sorry, Helga, wherever you may be, for the pain I caused you when you were young!"

Yet, that would be far too easy, *nicht var*?

The truly odd thing is that I operated during the entire episode strictly according to the advice of the Brawley family expert on such matters, which I had obtained when she made a brief visit to California during Helga's pregnancy. "Girls," said Grandma Florence, shaking her mottled neck (yet still a very handsome woman in her seventies), "they like to trap a man like that. If you don't love her, Ernie, leave her. She'll do nothing but bring you down."

As for our child (a man of sixty-two years old now), I never looked him up, though he was born in California where the records in such cases were declared open to the public long ago.

He never looked me up either.

Chapter Six

*No temptation can ever be measured
by the value of its object.*
COLLETE, 1966

One morning in 1962, I woke to the overpowering odor of cow shit, with no clue where I was, or how I got there. As I lay there in my sleeping bag, holding my nose, trying to put it all together, the sun popped out from behind a pair of chocolate-colored mountains, flared across a great desert valley, glinted through some wood slats, and hit me smack in the eye. After regaining my sight, I found myself lying in a sidetracked cattle car in a vast field of green tomatoes.

Slithering out of my sleeping bag, I heaved it and my backpack from the rail car, leapt to the track, and beat the dried dung off them with one of my boots. Then I staggered down the embankment and squatted by an irrigation canal to splash water on my face. Refreshed at last, I rose, shaded my eyes from the sun, and scanned the brightening horizon.

"IMPERIAL VALLEY AGRO," said a sign round a water tower in the distance.

And it all came back. Only three days before, I had walked off my job at San Quentin Prison and departed the Bay Area on my trip around the world.

Later that morning, organized at last, I stepped out on the road beside the tracks and started hitchhiking again. Somewhere along the line I had lost my "Around the World Backwards" sign.

My first ride was a mile down the road in a battered, green Chevy with an eighty-year-old Mexican irrigator with a white, Pancho Villa mustache. My second was in to the town of Brawley (no relation) with a family of Okie date pickers. But my third ride was solid glamour: a brand-new Cadillac Coupe de Ville with a palomino gold paint job, a *Hollywood, City of the Stars* license-plate frame, and a California State Bar Association decal in the rear window.

I sprinted through a billowing cloud of white dust to catch it. Yet, by the time I reached the Caddy, the cloud had blown away, leaving it miraculously dustless, and lustrous, in the sunshine.

Smiling courteously, I leaned in the window, and the couple inside turned to smile back.

The woman's smile was perfunctory, professional, but the man's was enormous, shark-toothed, dazzling.

A tall, suntanned blonde, she was a knockout in black, capri pants and a white, low-necked, cashmere sweater.

The guy was wearing a pair of grey slacks, a long-sleeved black shirt, and a grey fedora. Tall, thin, very dark, he had an eagle beak, a Clark Gable mustache, and heavily lidded eyes.

To me, they looked a bit bigger than life. But, hey, they were just what you might expect, riding out here in the middle of the desert, in a car like that, in this wild and wacky state of California.

They had a Los Angeles R & B station on the radio, "The Johnny Otis Show."

Johnny Otis, bop bop bop . . .
Johnny Otis, bop bop bop . . .

"Where you headed, honcho?" the driver wanted to know.

"Short-term or long-term?"

"Why don't you just lay it out for me, man?"

"Well, my immediate goal is Mexico," I replied. "But eventually, I want to go all the way around the world backwards."

"What do you mean by backwards?"

"It'll take a while to explain."

"Cool," he said, smiling brilliantly. "Hop in, buddy. You're a man after my own heart."

Truth is, I wasn't sure what I meant by "around the world backwards." Just seemed like an interesting theme for my journey, the meaning of which might sort itself out as I went along. And I figured that my varying replies to the inevitable question would be an interesting conversation opener with people who picked me up along the way.

Now, from the perspective of sixty-two years, I realize that my whimsical notion of going around the world backwards was in fact a kind of self-fulfilling prophecy, the meaning of which was symbolic rather than factual: By going around the world backwards, I hoped to find myself somewhere along the way.

The driver's girlfriend scooted over. I swung the door open and settled beside her in the front seat. Instantly, my pulse jumped. I tried not to stare but could not prevent myself from gaping in wonder. Her face was an adolescent fantasy. Her body instant cheesecake. I could not place her scent, but it smelled marvelous, smelled... warm. *She* was warm. I felt her body heat right through my Levi jacket.

Little Eva came on the radio then, singing, *"Come on, baby, do the Loco-Motion."*

"Tell me," said the driver, easing back out into traffic, forgetting—to my great relief, since I'd temporarily run out of inventive explanations—to ask me what I meant about going around the world backwards, "what's the best way to Guaymas and points south?"

"Well," I responded, "the guy who gave me my last ride? He says there's two ways. You can cross the border at Mexicali and take Mexican National 2 to Santa Ana. Or you can take U.S. 89 to Nogales, and Mexican National 15 straight down."

"Don't be coy, man, just tell me the fuckin' way."

"Okay, the guy said you ought to stay on the U.S. side as long as you can. You lose half a day by taking the Mexican route."

"Why didn't you just say that in the first place?"

"But you already knew all about it, Sam," the woman put in. "You swore last year you'd never take that Route 2 again."

Her voice was soft, melodious, slightly breathless, her accent cultivated, mid-Atlantic. She was an actor, of course.

"I did?" he said.

"You know you did."

"Just testing."

"You're always testing," she sniffed.

"Hey, I don't want to hear any more shit from you!" Sam growled, jabbing a finger in her face.

The gesture seemed so overblown, uncalled-for, that I felt unsure whether to take it seriously or not.

I took my cue from the woman; she ignored it.

"And you, honcho, what's so fucking funny?" Sam demanded.

"Nothing," I said, smothering a grin.

"You speak the lingo?"

"Pretty good."

"How come?"

"My dad's people speak it. Originally, they're from Ures, Sonora, so I guess I picked it up from them."

"How you fixed for bread?"

"Not so good."

"I pride myself on my ability to read character," Sam said, reaching into the glove compartment, pulling out a joint, lighting up. "Consider yourself on retainer, honcho, till further notice."

"You serious?"

"Never say anything I don't mean," he said, flashing a grin at me.

"Uh . . . well, thanks. Glad to be of service."

"Don't mention it. You smoke dope?"

"Don't turn it down."

"Try this stuff, man, you'll like it."

"Nice," I breathed, after a puff or two.

"One of my clients gave it to me," he said, smiling at the memory. "In lieu of payment."

"Here," I offered, handing it to the woman.

"The name's Maggie," she replied, dragging deeply, her breasts swelling under the cashmere. "Maggie Wells."

Without vanity, she said it. Although it was clear that she expected me to recognize her name. Which I didn't. But I did recall that face from somewhere, some TV drama or something back in the 'fifties. Those great smoldering dark eyes, so unusual in a true blonde, and those jutting cheekbones, the puffy bruised-looking lips, the flaring nostrils.

"Mine's Ernie. Ernie Brawley," I said, but wasn't sure she caught it.

"How'd you get a name like Brawley," Sam wanted to know, "if you're Spick?"

"Long story," I replied. "You sure you want to hear it?"

"I'm exhausted," Maggie yawned, stretching provocatively. "We left Malibu at five this morning."

A minute later, her head dropped to my shoulder, and she fell fast asleep.

"Don't get your balls in an uproar, man," Sam laughed, when he caught my anxious look. "I ain't the jealous type."

But I was not convinced. It was all too sudden. I did not know what to make of these people. All sorts of paranoid fantasies crossed my mind.

"If you see Rosamary," sang Fats Domino, *"tell 'er I'm comin' home to stay."*

In El Centro, Maggie rolled into the back seat.

Sam turned left onto Highway 8, heading southeast.

Soon, the vivid, green fields of winter vegetables ended, and the ribbon of blacktop sliced clean through a region of enormous white sand dunes.

"This is where they make all the Foreign Legion flicks," I remarked, but Sam did not seem interested.

What fascinated him was the sound of his own voice.

"Lemme tell you a story, man; you are not gonna believe this one. . . ."

What he needed was a sounding board, and I, the hitchhiker, was it.

For hours, the big dude wheeled his great, long Cadillac across the desert, telling tales. In a hoarse confidential tone, he told them, as if the telling itself were somehow illegal or unethical.

All my life people have come to me this way, to bend my ear. It was just as true then as it is now. They confess things to me they would not tell their best friends. There is something about me that encourages them to open up. What it is exactly, I haven't a clue. Fact is, I do not normally enjoy hearing these confessions, even though—as a writer—I should latch right onto them, use them in my work. Yet, the truth is that they make me feel uneasy, as if I am entrusted with someone's precious, fragile possessions. Also, I instinctively mistrust anyone who opens himself up to strangers. It's a natural reflex of the Mexican in me: "Never turn your back on a man who talks too much," my father used to say.

But this dude, he sure could spin a yarn. I could not deny him that. A brilliant raconteur, he dared to begin his stories in the middle or the end. Then flesh them out with intricately woven flashbacks. Or cut them off just before the climax. Or take them up in the middle of another story, merely to increase suspense. He told them in no apparent order, chronological or otherwise, but eventually a pattern emerged.

It was the story of his life:

"... So, Sam the Man, he finds himself rounding the corner of Hollywood and Vine. The city is basking in the first golden rays of the sun, but Sam, he cannot say the same for his wallet, see. The morning itself is holding him up. Then, just when things seem bleakest, up pulls Vito Palermo in a brand-new Continental. 'Hey, goombah,' he says, 'how's about helpin' me count some loot?' End of story. It's all a game. Already things are looking up...."

A few miles outside of Yuma, he suddenly yawned, quit talking right in the middle of one of his stories, and guided the Caddy to a slow smooth stop by the side of the road.

"How's about a spell at the wheel, honcho?"

"Sure," I said. "Why not?"

He rousted Maggie out of the back, we all stepped out to stretch our legs, then Sam and Maggie traded seats. Apparently, they were no longer speaking.

I slipped behind the wheel and hit the gas.

"Wake me up in Tucson," Sam yawned, then fell right off. His snoring was like everything else about him: loud, unabashed, with music all its own.

Although I can be as affable as an Irishman, I sometimes find myself unaccountably affected by the natural reserve of my Mexican side. Which was probably why I was feeling a bit shy... alone in the front seat with a movie star.

Anyway, Maggie seemed lost in her own thoughts, so we drove all the way across the Yuma Desert before we said a word.

Maggie said it: "Joint?"

"Sure," I nodded, and she rolled us a fat one.

We smoked silently, passing it back and forth.

Done, we turned to smile at each other.

"Yeah," she sighed, shaking her head.

"Yeah," I said, nodding.

After that, I figured we had established a kind of rapport, though we spoke not another word for the rest of the journey, and she slept most of the way.

At 6:00 p.m. we crossed the Mexican border.

A warm, pleasant evening in late spring with the sun hovering just over the bleached brick buildings, wind-burnt willows, and jagged desert foothills of Nogales.

The Avenida Juárez was crowded with commercial traffic: pushcart vendors hawking their wares, battered, old, pickup trucks, ranch wagons revving their engines, huge international semi-trailers spewing diesel smoke, great long Greyhound-style Mexican buses with their company insignia painted along their outside panels—*Norte de Sonora, Tres Estrellas de Oro, La Flecha Roja.*

The sidewalks spilled over with motley humanity: Indians with long Apache hair, *braceros* in straw sombreros, red-faced Arizonians in baseball caps or flower-print dresses, *vaqueros* in black Stetson hats, railroad men in bibbed overalls, local *pachucos* in grease-stained zoot suits.

It was good to be in the land of my ancestors. My pulse jumped to catch the Latin beat. Yet, I could die of humiliation at seeing my *part-raza* so, in dark, squalid contradiction to that scrubbed white behemoth to the north.

Sam parked the Caddy on a side street.

"Watch the wagon for me, will you, honcho," he said, "while me and the little missus rustle us up a hotel for the night."

Maggie did not take kindly to his humor.

He seemed to resent her lack of appreciation.

They ignored each other as they headed off down the street but managed to create a sensation anyway.

Sam had a way of swaggering, loose-limbed, cocksure, with his fedora pulled down over his eyes, which caught the attention of passersby.

Maggie on the other hand was so silky she seemed to glide down the street. Her movements, like her accent, were slightly stylized. Yet, the more I was around her, the more I came to believe that she was really like that. The style originated in her training as an actor, but by now it seemed to be second nature. I was no longer an objective observer, however, for already I was a little in love.

Shortly after they disappeared into the crowd, I noticed a twenty-dollar bill which had slipped out of Sam's pocket onto the backseat. I reflected on it for a moment, deciding that under certain conditions twenty dollars could mean the difference between life and death. I was about to reach for it when it occurred to me that Sam might have planted it there on purpose, as some kind of test.

The Hotel Paraíso, where we found accommodations for the night, was a newish, three-story, cinder block building located on the extreme southeastern edge of Nogales, across the street from an abandoned wool warehouse. Out back, there was a surprisingly well-tended little cactus garden, with a fishpond, a bed of colorful desert flowers, and a couple of honeymoon cottages. The rear of the property looked out onto the open desert. It was protected on three sides by a windbreak of junipers and tall, old, cottonwood trees with silvery leaves.

Sam rented the honeymoon cottages for the night. We all had a siesta, and at nine o'clock, Sam came around to my cottage and let himself in. Dressed for dinner, he wore a tan, lightweight suit, an open-neck black shirt, a Panama hat, and looked like a million pesos.

"Lemme explain the deal," he said. "Dig it, man, someone's gotta stick with those bags, whether it's in the hotel or when we're out on the road. I got cameras. I got travelers' checks. I got some cash. No offense, but my experience is that your people will steal. So, I want you here with the bags till we get back. Then you can run and grab a bite. All right?"

"No problem," I nodded, too proud to mention my own ravenous hunger, or the fact the room service could send out a meal in a jiffy.

So, I sat in their cottage till late that night, trying to keep my mind off food by drinking lots of water and going through their things. Two of the bags were open, full of personal effects like maps, clothing, cameras, toilet articles. But another bag—by far the largest—was double locked. I deduced that the loot was in this bag, and there was much more of it than Sam had admitted. It even occurred to me that I might steal the bags and disappear with them into the desert. But by ten o'clock I was reduced to pilfering Maggie's barbiturates, just to kill the hunger pangs.

Toward midnight, Sam came stomping in alone, fuming: "Fuckin' cunts. They're like Spooks, man. Give 'em an inch and they take a fuckin' mile."

Again, the queasy, uneasy feeling: Why was this guy confiding in me? Did he have something up his sleeve?

Sam threw himself down on the bed, reached for his dope, and there was something about the way he moved that increased my queasiness.

I found Maggie in the hotel bar, seated alone, sipping a margarita through a straw, listening to Bobby Rydell singing *"The Cha Cha Cha"* on the jukebox.

I sat beside her and asked the bartender if the kitchen had closed yet. It was, he said, but there was a place down the road that stayed open till two in the morning.

"Care to come along?" I asked Maggie.

"Why not?" she replied, smiling, stepping down off the bar stool.

Barelegged, wearing a peasant blouse with a red skirt, she staggered slightly when she hit the floor, rustling her skirt. But her recovery was so smooth, so nonchalant, it might have been taken for a graceful little parody of tipsiness, rather than the thing itself.

"Oh, you haven't got any money, have you, dear?"

"Afraid not," I said, shaking my head.

"I've got some."

"Thank you, but I'd like some company too."

"Any company?" she asked, flashing a smile.

"Yours, in particular," I responded, grinning back at her.

"Must stay out till Sam's asleep. Had a bit of a row."

"Nothing serious, I hope," I said, guiding her out of the hotel.

"Oh, it'll blow over in a day or two. I'm not even cross at him anymore. It's Sam now. He's cross because I was cross. If you know what I mean."

"Sort of."

"Rather enjoys his little fits of anger, you see. Part of his act."

"What act?"

"You know, the tough-guy act."

"Could've fooled me," I said. "But he sure can tell a story."

"Bit tiresome..." she sighed, shaking her head. "Once you've heard them a few times. I've never understood Sam's romance with the underworld. Sometimes, I think he's suffering from a case of 'arrested development,' like some of his clients. And I do tend to get onto him about it, from time to time."

"So that's what it was all about!"

"What?"

"Today," I said.

"Oh, no," she replied. "It was over you."

"Me?"

"To be perfectly frank, Ernie, I didn't want him to pick you up."

"Why not?"

"It was just once too often. That's all."

"You mean he does this a lot?"

"Oh, God yes! Must have his entourage, you see. Likes a good thick plot. The more confusion the better. Collects people the way you might collect potted plants. Some of the most unsavory types. And he just loves having them on."

"Pardon me?"

"You know. Always trying to find the weak point," she went on. "Always trying to keep one off balance. He does it with me all the time. But you won't let him intimidate you, will you, Ernie?"

"Well," I laughed, as if it were the remotest possibility in the world, "I'll try not to."

"His bark is far worse than his bite; I can assure you of that," she said, and she seemed quite serious. There was something about Maggie that seemed valid and guileless, despite everything. "Anyway, you don't fit the mold, do you?"

"What mold?"

"You know, the types he picks up."

"Well, thank you very much!" I chortled, but she didn't appear to catch my irony.

"No, you're not like all the rest, are you, Ernie?"

"I don't think so."

"You're cute," she whispered, leaning on my arm. "Nice."

For a guy who'd woken up in a cattle car not long before, I was doing all right. Yet, by no means had I dropped my guard: *What do these people want from me? What are their true intentions?*

We marched down the dusty road through the desert for a kilometer or so till we found an open-air restaurant on the main highway. It catered to truck drivers and busloads of *braceros*, and everyone made a big fuss over Maggie. The Mexican food was good, the beer cold, and I could fend off the more importunate of curious onlookers with occasional blasts of foulmouthed Spanish.

"Some appetite you've got there," Maggie observed, when I'd come to the end of my mountainous serving of *carne asado*, rice and beans.

"Been a while since I last ate."

"Gathered as much."

"Yeah."

"You're not quite who you say you are. Are you, Ernie?"

"Not quite," I snickered. "But then again, I guess none of us are. Are we, Maggie?"

"Suppose not. But you know..." she said, shaking her head, "I sometimes wonder if my entire history isn't just written smack across my face."

"It's a beautiful face!"

"Well, that's the point, isn't it?"

"I saw you a couple of times on TV, Maggie. You were great."

"Was I? Well, yes, I suppose I was."

"You were!"

"It never got me anywhere, though. Now here I am pushing forty."

"Jesus!" I scoffed. "Could've fooled me."

We strolled back to the hotel arm in arm, under a million twinkling desert stars, singing *"It Happened in Monterey"* together, in the style of Frank Sinatra, at the tops of our lungs.

At her cottage, she kissed me good night on the mouth. "You're a good sport, kid," she whispered in my ear.

Next morning, Maggie and Sam were still barely speaking.

Maggie reclined in the backseat of the Caddy, sometimes sleeping, sometimes smoking, sometimes reading an Agatha Christie mystery.

Sam took the wheel and all the way across the Sonora Desert the rap continued, just as seamless and beguiling as ever:

"... So, the Di Giovanni clan, they finally caught up with my old man, see? Slipped a pair of cement shoes on his feet and dumped him off the Santa Monica Pier. And my ma? She goes like bananas. They strapped her in a straitjacket, hauled her off to the bin. End of story. It's all a game. At the ripe age of thirteen, Sam became The Man...."

The higher Sam got, the more deeply involved in his interwoven stories, the broader his grin got. It was a devastating grin, at once cynical, mocking, and exultant, yet it had the continual effect of making me feel nervous—ill-at-ease. Also, Sam leaned too close when he wanted to pursue a point and touched me on the knee too often.

I began to develop paranoid thoughts: The macho talk was all a front. The dude was a closet queen and Maggie his shill.

Yet, even paranoia did nothing to diminish the fascination I felt for Sam. I'd never met anyone remotely like him. He was so big, so loud, so brash, so overwhelming as a personality that I became aware of a kind of shrinking within myself, a retreat of my manhood.

I realized that the dope was coloring my perceptions, but there seemed little I could do to prevent it. It did no good to laugh at Sam for foolishly running off at the mouth, for revealing his most intimate secrets to a stranger, because I could not deny that the rendition itself was marvelously exciting.

I began to sweat. Got the shakes. Maggie receded into the background. It was just Sam and me, in the saddle of that great palomino, galloping across the Mexican desert. . . .

I gazed longingly out the window, daydreaming of escape into the *Sierra de Batuc* or the *Desierto del Altar*. . . .

"Hey, what's happenin', honcho?" Sam wanted to know.

"Not much," I replied, jerking my head up and down.

"Looked like you drifted off there for a bit."

"Maybe."

"You know what, my man? You're a good-lookin' kid, but you're too like . . . *sensitivo*. Lookin' a little green around the gills. You know what I'm a sayin'?"

"I'll be all right!" I retorted. But in my weakness, I felt compelled to check myself, to reconfirm my own masculinity, much as I had done in college with my sexual conquests.

And by the time we got to Hermosillo, the sweltering capital of Sonora, I had just about decided I was going to let my native fever have its way with me again. I would have Sam's lady somewhere along the line. Just to prove that I could do it. Just to cut this big fucker down to size.

Across a plain as flat and featureless as any on earth, the shimmering Sea of Cortéz appeared before us, and an hour later we pulled into Guaymas, Sonora, a grimy, little, shrimp-fishing port on Bocochibampo Bay.

Sam drove across to the beach side—called Miramar—and I stayed in the car while Sam and Maggie stepped out to look for a hotel. The couple was still not speaking and ignored each other as they had the day before.

They found a *modernistico* little place at the far end of the beach, then signaled me to drive down to meet them. I was tempted to drive right past them, straight down the road to Mazatlan, but I did as I was bid.

Sam got us adjoining rooms on the third floor of the hotel, overlooking the sea. At dinnertime, I was left alone with the bags again. Sam came in about midnight, threw off his clothes, and fell on the bed. It was like the patter he laid down every day sapped his energy, and he hadn't much left over at night.

"So, what're you waiting for, man?" he wanted to know.

"Yeah. Guess I'll go and get something to eat."

"Unless you got something else on your mind."

"What?"

"Go ahead," Sam sniffed, waving me out of the room. "I'm gonna smoke some weed and crash."

I found Maggie at the bar, slightly tipsy, delighted to see me. The hotel kitchen was closed, so we took a stroll down the beach to an open-air restaurant where I gorged myself on tortillas, guacamole, beer, and *Huachinango a la Veracruzana*.

Maggie was bare legged again, barefoot, with her espadrilles dangling from her pinky finger. And by then, I had convinced myself that I was more than a little in love.

On the way back to the hotel, we sat on a pile of fresh sawdust, near the whale-like skeleton of a half-constructed tuna boat, to smoke a doobie. We sat quietly, watching the little curls of waves, the phosphorescence in the water, and the moon as it rose over the *Estero del Río Muerto*.

"Come on!" Maggie cried, leaping to her feet.

"What?"

"How about a moonlight swim?"

We stripped to our underwear, hung our clothes on the spars of a fishing boat, raced across the beach, and plunged into the waves, which we found amazingly warm, sticky with brine.

"Let's go!" she shrieked. "Let's go way, way out!"

We swam all the way to Point Kino and back. When our feet found sand again, we came together in the water. She was slippery in my arms and tasted like salt. I ran my hands down the curve of her hips and buttocks. Started to slip her panties down.

"No . . ." she moaned, pressing herself to me. "No!"

She broke away, ran for the beach. I sprinted after her, kicking spray, and caught her in the shallows. We fell in a heap, kissing again, thrusting at each other instinctively, rolling in the sand.

"No, no, no . . ." Maggie kept saying.

Was the show of resistance meant to be overcome, or what?

She escaped my arms, crawled out of the water, and raced for her clothes, her body sleek and undulant in the moonlight.

We dressed and smoked some more *mota* by the fishing boat while our clothes dried.

A couple of times I was tempted to throw her down in sawdust, but all we did was engage in small talk.

"Suppose you wonder why he trusts you so much," Maggie said on the way back to the hotel.

"It has occurred to me."

"Part of the pattern. He does it with everyone, even his law partner. It's not that he really trusts people. He just likes to throw temptation at them, see how they react."

"What for?"

"Fucked if I know. All part of the test, I guess."

"How long have you been together?"

"Not long," she said. "Caught me at a weak moment. Hadn't a clue what I was getting into. Then I suppose it was simply that no one else came along. I have no one to rely on, you see."

"You can rely on me."

"Oh, Ernie, you're sweet. But you're too young."

"I'm old enough."

"Are you? I fancy you are. But you haven't got any money, have you?"

"I will have, someday. I'm gonna be a writer!"

"A writer? Haha! You'll never support a woman on a writer's salary. God preserve us from the arts! I ought to know. And besides, I'm sick of stories. Got 'em coming out of my ears."

"Are they true, do you think?"

"Never been able to find out one way or the other."

"No idea?"

"I can only judge by the way he acts."

"How does he act?"

"He has fantasies, Ernie. Action, drama, mystery . . . part of the hoodlum act. I mean, he likes to pretend he's this ethnic Italian, but I happen to know that his mother was Jewish.

"I'll give you another example of what I mean. He's got a very lucrative law practice, but probably half his clients are dope dealers who refuse to pay him in anything but cash. Since most of it is un-traceable, Sam pockets it without declaring it to the IRS. Every year or so, when his wall safe overflows, he packs a suitcase full of money, carries it out of the country. Deposits it in this secret numbered account he's got in some Panamanian bank down in Acapulco. He doesn't really need to do all this, you see. He makes more than enough money above the board, yah? And it's stupid as well, I should think, because eventually the IRS is going to catch up with him. But he loves his 'caper,' as he calls it, and he wouldn't give it up for the world. I think in his daydreams he sees himself as an international wheeler-dealer, a Mafia don or something."

"So, why don't we do him a favor, then?" I asked. It just popped out. I had no intention of saying any such thing.

"What?"

"Why don't we steal it?"

"You're kidding, of course."

"You think so?"

"Still," she said, laughing, "wouldn't it be something? Serve him right, as well. Oh Lord, what I wouldn't give to see his face. And I wouldn't feel a qualm, you know. He bloody well owes me. For sitting there listening to him all these months."

Later, after Maggie had gone off to her room, I could hear her and Sam whispering through the wall.

"You get it on with the kid?"

"None of your business."

"I make it my business."

"You're a nasty business, Sam."

"That's right!" he snorted. "I'd like to watch. And then I'd like to fuck you both."

I was treated to the next installment of the endless Sam the Man Story in the morning, on the desolate *Llanura Costera* between Guaymas and Navajoa, while Maggie napped in back:

"... So, Maggie walks in the office, man, and instantly I dig she's been beat for the yolk. I try to figure some way to get 'em on breach of contract, but it's no good. As a financial proposition, the broad is a total loss. As a movie queen, she's all washed up. End of story. It's all a game. I take her in out of the goodness of my heart and..."

"I thought the lawyer-client relationship was supposed to be confidential," Maggie interjected, waking from her nap.

"Glad you reminded me of that."

"Must've slipped your mind."

"Won't let it happen again," Sam said, "if you don't."

"What's that supposed to mean?"

"The rules of confidentiality. They apply to you just as they apply to me."

"You been sneaking around again, Sam? Sticking your nose where you hadn't ought?"

"Any more shit from you, bitch, and you go out!"

"Right, you're the captain of the ship."

"Believe it!"

"Just keep talking, Sam. That's what you're good at."

"When the talk stops," he snarled. "That's when you gotta look out."

"Never known it to stop yet," Maggie retorted, to his immense annoyance.

A few seconds later, at a sign that said, *"Selva de Cactus,"* Sam swung off the main highway, and headed up a dirt road toward a forest of giant Saguaro cactus trees spread across the lower slopes of a high flat mesa.

He drove into the middle of the forest and pulled to a stop.

"Get out, bitch!"

"What for?"

"I'm gonna fuckin' murder you! Never mind for what. Get out."

Reluctantly, Maggie climbed out of the backseat.

Sam pulled a blanket from the trunk and joined her by the side of the car. "Come with me," he ordered.

"Where we going?"

"I'm gonna fuck you in the ass."

"Oh no you're not!"

"Wanna bet?" he said.

"Yeah!" she shrieked and kicked him in the shin with the sharp toe of her high-heeled sandal.

Sam dropped the blanket, wound up, and slapped her across the face, hard, knocking her to the ground.

Crying, trying to gather her breath, Maggie struggled to rise.

If she had called out, or even looked my way, I would have gone to her aid. But the way things were, I figured it was something between the two of them. Also, there was something ritualistic in this passionate exchange which led me to believe that there had been other such dramas in the past.

Sam picked up the blanket and jerked her to her feet.

"No, I don't want to!" she screamed.

"You don't know what you want," he scoffed, dragging her off into the cactus. "I gotta *show* you what you want."

"I don't want this!"

"You do."

"I don't!"

"Then I'll *take* it!" he sniggered.

Maggie fought him all the way 'till he got her panties down. The silence of the desert was so profound that I could hear everything.

Her surrender was magnificent.

As soon as it was over, though, I could hear Maggie shrieking at him again.

But that didn't stop him from doing it to her again.

Halfway through the second session, I couldn't take it anymore. Figured it was either drop the Caddy in low and disappear with the loot or pound my pud. The thing that tipped the scales was I thought I heard air escaping. I'd look ridiculous trying to run off with a flat tire, wouldn't I?

Later, after I'd whipped it off and smoked some more dope, I noticed that another twenty-dollar bill had dropped to the floor on the driver's side. After thinking about it for a while I finally decided to take it. I figured it was part of my retainer.

Then suddenly I felt very, very high, and entered the heart of the falcon, flying a thousand feet above the desert. I watched the Hollywood couple fighting and fucking in the Saguaro Forest, the Caddy parked on the white dirt road, the faithful but furtive little retainer inside, groping on the floor for the twenty-dollar bill that the *patrón* had dropped.

"Bullshit!" I hollered and jumped out of the car.

Checking the left rear tire, I found that it had indeed gone flat. Opening the trunk, I pulled out the jack, the spare, and set about methodically changing the tire. It seemed to take a hundred years. As I was finishing, I could hear the lovers walking back through the cactus.

"I hate you, Sam!"

"All I do is show you what you are, Maggie."

"You make me less than I am," she sniffled. "You've got a talent for that."

I put away the flat tire and jack, then climbed in behind the wheel.

"Where you goin', honcho?" Sam wanted to know.

"Mind if I drive?" I inquired, smiling politely.

"Naw. Thanks for changing the flat."

"Nothing to it. We'll have to stop in Navajoa to get it fixed, though. These roads are murder on tires."

Sam crawled in back, fell right to sleep.

Maggie sat in front, shamefaced, pretending to look out the window.

I bided my time. About an hour out of Navajoa, Sam woke up, said he had to take a leak. He got out, headed down the embankment, and unzipped his pants.

I waited till he had it out, then stepped on the gas.

"Hey!" he bellowed, with his dick in his hand. "Where the fuck you think you're going?"

"He's got a good question there," Maggie observed, laughing, watching her boyfriend recede into the dust.

"Haven't given it much thought," I responded, smiling, shaking my head.

"Mind if I come along for the ride?" she asked.

We ditched the car in Navajoa, took a train to Mazatlán. On the way I didn't have much to say. I was a bit shocked at what I'd done.

Maggie, on the other hand, stayed high, and it was hard to tell how she felt, one way or the other.

Arriving in Mazatlán late that night, we checked our bags at the station, caught a taxi to the central plaza. As it happened, it was fiesta time, the feast day of the city's patron saint, and the town was jumping.

That is to say, the upper classes of the locality had hired some mariachi bands, tanked themselves up on tequila, and were living it up in the bars that line the *malecón*, while the poor—the vast majority of the population—looked on in solemn disbelief, or attempted to sell them trinkets.

But Maggie and I were adopted by a young, German Mexican brewer and his wife and were swept about the wealthier sections of the town in a whirlwind of party-going. Though the gaiety was frantic, the dancing and drinking wild and abandoned, neither Maggie nor I felt much like partaking. We allowed ourselves to be led around, introduced, displayed, chatted to, danced with, without really feeling much. In fact, we were overcome with a kind of fatal inertia, as if we were merely waiting for Sam, or the law, to catch up with us.

Dawn found us strolling along the public beach at Olas Altas, barefoot, hung over.

We walked out to the end of the breakwater to catch a little breeze and spotted a Xixime couple from the mountains. They were sitting on a rock, cross-legged, in native costume. They had a huge pile of marijuana in front of them, and they were sorting the stems from the leaves.

The man smiled at Maggie and me, then asked if we'd like to sample his wares.

I said we would be delighted, but we didn't have much cash.

The man replied, "*No importa*," and proceeded to roll us all a corn husk cigarette stuffed with his best *sinsemilla*.

We joined the natives on the rock, sat there smoking with them for most of the morning, chatting about the weather, the boats on the water, and the porpoises we could see bubbling in the channel.

By noon we were wasted. We could barely stand. But the Xixime couple had not once shifted their position on the rock or ceased their skillful culling of the stems from the leaves.

"Bye-bye," said Maggie, rising to her feet, preparing to go.

"For the road," the man said, and solemnly bestowed upon her a half-kilo of *mota* in a cornmeal sack.

"*Muchas Gracias*," I said, and guided Maggie slowly, unsteadily back to the city.

We caught a taxi to the railway station and retrieved a couple of bags, including the one with Sam's loot. On a lark, we agreed to take the first train that came along, no matter which way it was going. As it happened, it was bound for Guadalajara. We found a couple of seats in first class, curled up, and didn't know a thing until the train reached Guadalajara Central, at eight o'clock that night.

We left the train, rolled ourselves a fat one in the parking lot, and started again where we had left off in the morning. This time, the first train that came along was the Colima Express. It was packed, but we found a space in a third-class car full of Mexican Army soldiers. Weighed down with combat gear, including loaded M-1 rifles and twelve-inch bayonets, they were heading out to evict a band of militant squatters from a rich landowner's property.

As the train rolled out of Guadalajara, winding its way into the mountains, the soldiers began sniffing the air, exchanging glances.

"¿Qué es esto?"

"¿Mota?"

"¡Que sí!"

"¿Quien tiene la mota?"

"What's going on?" Maggie wanted to know.

"It's our bag. They smell it."

"So, what do we do now?"

"We offer them some, if we're smart," I said, and sent her over to pour a quarter-kilo into the corporal's kit bag.

"Muchas gracias, señorita."

"Don't mention it," she said in English, flashing her most photogenic smile.

For a while after that, everything was fine. The soldiers smoked, laughed, joked amongst themselves. They broke into their K rations to gorge themselves on Hershey chocolate. Someone pulled out a bottle of tequila and soon they were singing military songs. They sang *La Valentina, La Cucaracha, La Adelíta*, and others of lesser renown. The songs got louder, lewder, and presently the soldiers were ogling Maggie, inviting her to come over and ride on their laps.

"Maybe we ought to display a more neighborly spirit," I suggested.

"You think that'll do it, eh?" she scoffed. "All right, let's roll a couple of numbers and join the party."

"*Señores*, may I have the honor of presenting my wife?"

"*Encantado, señora, encantado* . . ."

The gesture of introducing my "wife" served to defuse some of the sexual tension, but it did nothing to diminish the noise level. In fact, Maggie's proximity tended to make them even more rambunctious. Soon, they were competing for her attention by firing their weapons out the windows, screaming, "*¡Muerte a los oficiales!* Death to the officers!"

And then, to uproarious laughter, "*¡Mátalos, mátalos!* Kill them! Kill them!"

The conductor came forward, tried to make them see reason, but when he encountered resistance—"*¡Mátalo, mátalo!*"—he withdrew to wire ahead for reinforcements.

When the train pulled into Tuxpán, a whole platoon of Azules, the dreaded head-cracking national police of Mexico, was drawn up on the station platform.

We exited from the other side of the car while the train was still in motion and made our way swiftly out of town.

Soon we found ourselves walking down a long, straight, white-sand road in the light of a full moon.

"Where we going?" Maggie wondered.

"Damned if I know," I replied.

"These bags are going to get heavy."

"You mind?"

"I don't know."

"I have never been higher in my life, Maggie."

"I've never felt closer to . . ." she began.

"God?"

"Death."

"Same thing," I said.

"Of course," she replied, and we laughed together in the silence.

Then the cacti around us melted and oozed into the cracks in the stone walls beside the road. Suddenly there were a million moons in the sky. The white road stretched away in the white moonlight to infinity. At the end of infinity was a tiny speck that grew larger, becoming a rural policeman riding a mule, with an old Springfield rifle resting on the pommel of his saddle.

We walked straight past him; not even sure he was real.

He wasn't sure that we were real, either. He blinked his eyes. Passed a hand over his face. Sniffed the air. Waited till we were fifty meters down the road before he could clear his voice to speak.

"¡*Alto!*" he shouted. "Stop!"

But we just kept on keeping on. The white road stretched out in front of us again between the cacti and the stone walls, into infinity.

"¡Alto, alto, alto!"

The voice kept getting smaller behind us. Finally, it became almost pathetic, almost begging us to stop.

"Alto, por favor . . ."

Then we heard the report of a rifle shot. The air cracked between us, then whistled away into the distance. The cacti quivered in fright and hid amid the rocks.

But Maggie and I just kept on walking, one foot ahead of the other, too high to die.

We hiked for another hour or so, till an apparition rose before us in the moonlight—a pair of tall conical mountains, one crowned with snow, the other spouting fire.

Without a word between us, we knew that this was our ultimate destination.

At the base of the volcano there was a sawmill, a lumberyard, and a small village—Atenquique. We woke the proprietor of the company store to rent a room for the night. In the morning, we found that a stone refuge hut existed high in the mountains, which could be rented for twenty pesos a night.

"Sam will never find us there!" Maggie giggled. "Not in a million years!"

We spent the day buying firewood, provisions, and arranging with the lumber company for a fifteen-day occupancy of the refuge hut. Next morning, we hired a guide, a couple of donkeys, and set out for the mountain. And we didn't stop until we had reached the stone house, on a saddle of black rock at nine thousand feet, between the fire and the snow.

We sent the guide and donkeys back to town. Watched the sun go down. Smoked some more dope—ate, drank, pissed, shit, fucked, slept.

The next day we took in the view. We could see a hundred miles in all directions. We could see Guadalajara, Cocula, Ciudad Guzmán, the lakes of Chapala and Zapotlán. We could see the entire state of Colima, including the coffee plantations on the slopes of the volcano, the capital city, the coastal banana plain, the harbor of Manzanillo, and the black Pacific littoral.

In the afternoon, we made love again, hungrily, then slept the dreamless sleep of the drugged. We sat up all night smoking dope, not talking, only touching. There was not a sound in the world but our own breathing—sometimes slow, sometimes fast. No people. No machines. No animals. No insects. No plants. No wind. No rain. The air was balmy and warm.

We stayed a fortnight on the mountain. When we came down, I knew little more about Maggie than I had when we came up. Yet, I was convinced I knew all there was to know.

Her real name was not Maggie Wells. It was Maya Kovaks. She was one-quarter Mohawk Indian, three-quarters Slovak, and hailed from Ottawa, Canada. She had a sunny disposition, a profound sense of humor, a special feeling for children, animals, poor folks, Mexicans, and Blacks. Her education was sketchy, her mental powers unremarkable. She had little curiosity, rarely came up with an idea of her own.

What she did was react. But she reacted beautifully, instinctively, playing my sounds right back at me, with an inspired little riff of her own at the end. Yet, appearances to the contrary, Maggie was not a shallow person. In fact, I found her to be very deep. As deep and empty as the Sea of Cortéz. So empty that she was . . . profound, like space. She was everywhere and nowhere. She was anything and everything. She was whatever I wanted her to be, and I knew she had been the same for Sam.

I wanted her sweet, she cooed like a dove. I wanted her salty, she nearly clawed my eyes out. She was a nature girl, a goddess of love.

Why else would they want to make her a movie star?

In the end, I grew to fear her: Without meaning to, with all the best intentions, she might swallow me up without a trace.

"It was great, wasn't it?" I said, when we caught the train for Guadalajara.

"Yes, it was," she replied. "I'll never forget it."

"Where you headed now, Maggie?"

"Home, I should think."

"Back to Sam?"

"For a while, perhaps. And you, Ernie?"

"Hey, I've barely started."

"Oh, of course, that's right!" she hooted. "You're on your way round the world backwards, aren't you? Well, you know, I'd be happy to share some of his money, love, but I'm afraid he'd kill me if I did."

"Don't even think about it, Maggie," I said. "I started with nothing. I'll probably end up with nothing. It's all part of the trip."

"Yes," she replied, laughing. "All part of the trip, isn't it? I like that."

"End of story," I said, laughing back. "It's all a game."

In Guadalajara, Maggie took a train north and I started hitching south. With her aggrieved lover, Sam, in mind, I traveled fast. In three days, I crossed over the Guatemalan border.

A quarter of a century later, I would use Maggie as the model for Val Raymond, the faded movie star in my novel, *The Alamo Tree*. I have no idea whether she read it or not. For years, I hoped she wouldn't, but by now I guess it doesn't matter much, since at a hundred years old she is either in her dotage, or in her grave.

Chapter Seven

They never taste who always drink.
MATHEW PRIOR, 1697

I had thought Central America would be hot and tropical, but Guatemala was not like that at all. It was cool, almost alpine, with fir trees, grassy meadows, high cliffs, hemp bridges swinging across deep gorges, and fields of maize planted two or three thousand feet up steep green mountains. The population was Indigenous of the Maya tribe.

Everyone went barefoot; there appeared to have been no change in their lives since before Columbus, except for the machetes, made in Chicago, that the men all wore at their waists.

One day, I was hitchhiking outside Huehuetenango in the Guatemalan highlands when up drove a tall, rangy, middle-aged American couple in a spiffy, new camper truck. They were the Schmidts, they said, from North Platte, Nebraska, headed for Guatemala City, and they would be delighted for my company.

I hopped in, then we crawled off down the rough, narrow, winding dirt road that proudly proclaimed itself every few kilometers as The Pan-American Highway.

Though kindly enough, Mr. Schmidt was incredibly talkative, neurotic, unable to focus on a subject for over ten seconds. When he stepped out to dribble in the bushes by the side of the road, Mrs. Schmidt nudged me. "The reason why he appears so strange," she whispered, "he has a fatal neurological disease, only got a few more years to live."

When he found out about the illness, she said, he sold their ranch in North Platte, bought the camper truck, and decided to see the world before he was bedridden for the few remaining years of his life. As for Mrs. Schmidt, she had no interest in travel at all: "I'm only along for the ride."

About an hour out from Huehuetenango, near the town of Totonica, a Volkswagen camper with New York plates had stopped by the side of the road. Near the door, in a greasy, pinstripe suit and a filthy white polo shirt, beckoning to us frantically, stood a swarthy, crop-haired, little man with the sharp-nosed, chinless face, the quick, furtive movements of a rodent... and a left eye that wandered about in no apparent coordination with the right.

"Hi, I'm Ray. Ray Minelli. Listen, you know what? A rock just split my oil pan," he blared, in a Brooklyn accent so thick and vulgar that it sounded almost theatrical. "And, like, hey, could you tow a fellow *gringo* into the next town?"

The Schmidts agreed to help.

Then, while the two older men busied themselves with the work of attaching the towrope, I turned toward Ray's companion—a young, pretty *mestiza* who had just stepped out of the van. Wondering how she happened to be traveling with this crass, middle-aged American, I gave her the once over, and she stared boldly right back.

We were parked along a cliff that fell into a rushing stream.

Across the stream, a green mountain rose precipitously to a height of seven thousand feet. High rain clouds swelled above the mountain. An evening wind swept off the ridge, blowing the smell of fresh wet grass, pressing the girl's yellow summer dress against her brown thighs.

As the two American men chatted in the background about their towing job, I sniffed the air, filled my lungs, then looked again at this dark, exotic creature with the pouting red mouth.

This time, I made it a point to smile at her and shrug, as if inviting her complicity as a fellow young person amongst foolish adults. And the smile that she flashed in return, which lit up her entire face, caused my canine member to sit straight up in my pants, as if to beg for a bone.

Eventually, the Americans got the towing organized, then drove into Totonica. When they found a garage still open at 9 p.m., we all got out, and I stepped over to chat with the girl.

"*Pero que bien tu hablas castellano!*" she exclaimed, delightedly, in her Guatemalan Spanish. "But how well you speak Castillian!"

"*Soy de origen español,*" I replied with pride, though in fact I am only a quarter Mexican, and picked up Spanish working in the tomato fields as a kid in California.

As it turned out, her name was Celestina. The daughter of a Guatemalan customs officer, she had been to visit her father at the Mexican border, where he asked the American gentleman if he might carry her back to where she lived with her mother in Guatemala City.

Why he had entrusted his pretty daughter to such a disreputable-looking *gringo* I would never know.

She was seventeen but looked twenty, with a grave, polite, mature manner that made the brief flickering glances she sent my way even more entrancing.

"I want to ask you something," she said, after we had chatted for only a moment. "Could you accompany us in the van? I don't trust this man, Ray, and he has a *pistola*."

As it happened, I'd had my own strong reservations about Ray, ever since we saw him by the side of the road. On my journey through Mexico, I had run into several fugitives from justice, and he had the look. Yet, when his van had been repaired, I asked him if I could join him.

I did this for Celestina, despite my normally strong self-preservative instincts.

Later, I would blame it on my ancestral fever.

"Hey, no *problema*," Ray replied. Then a sly look crossed his smooth grayish face. "Thing is, man, I don't speak the lingo," he said, lowering his voice. "Can't get nowhere with this little broad. Maybe you . . . ?"

I sometimes found Ray's Brooklynese almost indecipherable, and it took me a while to understand what he meant by such phrases as *"da ting iz,"* and *"wit dis broawd."*

"Then what?" I managed at last.

"You ain't gonna keep her all to yourself, are you?"

"I'll see what I can do," I lied, for I liked Celestina; and I did not intend to feed his unhealthy appetites.

We waved goodbye to the Schmidts, and ten klicks down the road we pulled into a village with a fiesta going on. A *conjunto* of Maya tribe members stood in the bandbox at the center of the square, playing European instruments such as guitars, saxophones, trumpets, clarinets, and drums. Yet, the music they emitted was like no earthly sound I had ever heard.

Maya couples in their native costumes were dancing in the square, somberly, barely touching each other, and the crowd seemed amazingly quiet given the festive nature of the occasion.

Ray parked the van, and we all got out to order drinks at a kiosk.

After knocking back a few *copas* of the local firewater, a cane liquor called *aguardiente,* I began to find the strange, otherworldly syncopation of the Indian band rather catchy. I asked Celestina to dance, and she stepped into my arms, pressing her body to mine with such abandon that I realized the *aguardiente* was working on her, too.

Quickstepping about the slick tiles of the square, doing a hot, writhing, Latin *salsa*, we were good together, so good that everyone else in the plaza stopped dancing to stare at us. What I liked about Celestina was that she never smiled at me, never spoke, just let her body do the talking.

Despite the excellence of our performance, no one clapped when we left the plaza. No one said a word. Soon the Mayas were all silently dancing again, as if we had never been there at all.

Another hour down the road and Ray pulled off into a pine grove. "Too tired to drive anymore," he announced, stretching, yawning over-dramatically, winking at me with his one good eye. "Gonna take a blanket, throw it on the pine needles somewhere, try to get me some sleep...."

Celestina did not ask me what he had said. It was as self-evident as he intended it to be. Yet, the instant he scurried out of sight, she was in my arms. I found her cheap perfume, her sweaty body, her warm panting mouth that tasted like cane liquor, utterly captivating.

"Shall we get in back?" I asked.

I knew this was not in her best interests, especially when Ray was added to the equation, but the fever of my ancestors had me by the *cojones*, and there was no resisting it.

On his gamy, fetid mattress, I fell upon the girl like a beast of the night, gnawing at her tender lips, frail shoulders, and sparrow breasts while breathless she murmured my name in Spanish, "*Ernesto, Ernesto, Ernesto....*"

Up the yellow frock. Down the homespun cotton knickers. Nose to belly *that never bore a bastard*. Tongue to *omphalos*. Black thatch to flowery folds. Then dewier penetration. Oops! A web of opposition. *Virga intacta!*

With this marvel of marvels in mind, I rose from Celestina's virginal pudenda, grasped my bulging member, then ever so gently entered her, millimeter by millimeter, until she shrieked at me, "Just *do* it to me, Ernesto, *do* it!"

Instantly I obliged, rupturing her maidenhead with one great blood-spattered lunge. In an exquisite fusion of pleasure and pain, the girl wept, moaned, and cried my name.

"Ernesto, Ernesto!"

I sputtered into her almost immediately, howling my ecstasy at the moon . . . then glimpsed Ray standing just outside the van, one verminous eye glued wide to the rear window, the other wandering aimlessly about.

Even before our last reflexive pelvic thrusts had ceased, he swung the back door open, climbed in beside us, and unbuckled his belt.

"*Que no! ¡Te lo suplico, no!*" Celestina pleaded.

But there was no supplication in Ray; he had already hoisted her dress with one hand, pressed his gun in her ear with the other, and crawled aboard.

"*Por favor, no, no!*"

"*Celestina, no hay nada hacer,*" I whispered to her in Spanish, stroking her sweaty hair, as he thumped at her like a one-eyed rat. "There is nothing we can do. He has us out here in the middle of nowhere. He could pull the trigger if you resist."

On the way to Guatemala City, Celestina would not utter a word, would not look at me, no matter what I said.

"We don't wanna leave her off at her mother's place," Ray confided. "For sure, she gonna get hysterical, right? Then they call the cops. Gotta have time to sneak over the El Salvador border."

After taking a moment to translate his meaning, *Huh mudda place . . . Den dey coal da cops*, I silently concurred with his evaluation (let he without sin cast the first stone), for I feared we had no choice.

Therefore, when we made a piss stop at a gas station in Chemaltengo, Ray and I just pretended to go pee. We dropped Celestina's bag by the gas pumps while she was up in the pine grove that served as a lady's commode, then left her there alone, in the middle of the night, fifty long, hard miles from home.

I do not recall Celestina's facial features anymore, other than the fact that she was "pretty." Though I used her again as the shepherdess in my novel *Blood Moon* (as I have used nearly all the women in my life), her face has receded in my memory to the point where it has become a kind of generic *mestiza* face.

Even so, I have retained one thing from our brief encounter, besides undying shame and guilt and regret for my hereditary fever.

The way she said my name in Spanish, in her curious Guatemalan accent, sounded so good to me that I instantly shed the childish diminutive "Ernie," and I have been known forever since as "Ernesto."

Like my ancestors, therefore, and like my master, *ineluctably constructed upon the incertitude of the void,* I invented a brand-new self upon the fruitful field of my own distended ego, with a dash of pure random chance.

Next day, across the border in El Salvador, I was bodysurfing off Acajútla Beach when two big tiger sharks with dorsal fins like black sails cut me off from shore, then dawdled amid the shoals as if they had all the time in the world.

Treading water beyond the waves, wondering if they'd ever take it into their fishy brains to depart and allow my return to *terra firma,* I felt a surge of water against my swim fins, then found myself being drawn swiftly out to sea in one of the infamous riptides of this stretch of coast.

I knew better than to struggle against it. I went with the flow until it finally let up about a half mile from shore, from which point Ray and the fisher folk on the beach looked like a bunch of teeming ants. There was no use swimming against the tide, so I tried swimming around it: first to the right for a few hundred yards, then to the left; but everywhere the current was just too strong.

To ride out the surge, I rolled onto my back and tried to float, but the little, chopping waves and the wind-driven spray kept washing over my face, clogging my throat, my nostrils, preventing me from getting my breath. By then my arms and legs felt like dead weights, and for the first time I began to contemplate the possibility of divine retribution for my recent sins.

An hour later, when my lungs were filling with water, when my heart had nearly stopped from adrenalin fatigue, when Celestina in the guise of my Uncle Tom's boy, Tito Retoñito, had come back to taunt me—"¡Ven, ven, vente conmigo! Come, come with me"—when small, colorful carnivorous fish, sensing the inevitable, were already beginning to nibble at my fingers, I heard a putt-putting sound.

Then, off in the distance, I made out a little, one-man, fishing boat bobbing in the waves.

If I could just manage to raise my hand. . . .

But it was all I could do to keep my nose above the water.

Fortunately, the solitary fisherman, a wizened old *mestizo*, had eagle eyes. Spotting me from a long way off, he putt-putted over, grabbed me by the hair and hauled me aboard.

I lay gasping in the bottom of the boat beside his gnarled brown feet for half an hour, like a big, gaffed fish, until the sly demonic Tito/Celestina, still mouthing innuendos, finally disappeared into the ethos.

As we rounded the breakwater of the fishing port, I finally managed to raise my head to thank the wiry, wind-burnt little fellow for saving my life. But he just crinkled up his eyes and laughed.

"*Oye, señor.* Don't thank me. Thank the Lady."

"What lady?"

"The Lady of the Water," he said. "You weren't even swimming when I saw you. You were already dead, drowned, headed for the bottom. But swimming right there beside you, I could see her. Beautiful as a young girl she was, a dark virgin, holding you up, waving at me to sail over and bring you aboard. I tell you, *hombre,* without her personal intervention, you would be sleeping with the fishes now."

"Or worse," I said. For the implication of my watery lesson had not been lost on me.

And I wondered again at the supernal nexus of women.

Their infinite wiles.

The whimsy of their mercies.

The weightiness of their deterrent examples.

Later, in Honduras somewhere, after an all-night drinking binge, Ray divulged his surname to me and admitted that he was indeed "on the lam." He had bit his ex-wife's nipple off, he said, for fucking around with another man. It went septic, and she nearly died. Now he was bound for Nicaragua, which had no extradition treaty with the United States, where he intended to "lay low" till the heat was off.

I wasn't done with Ray yet, but perhaps the most astounding occurrence about the entire episode was this: Years later, while I was sitting cross-legged in front of the Toshoku Shrine in Nikko, Japan, with a prayer flag, a sign begging alms in English and Nipponese, and a bowl full of *yen* laid out in front of me, I ran into Mrs. Schmidt again.

Her husband had recently died in Indonesia, she said. Out of consideration for his memory, she had set about finishing his overland trip across all the inhabited places of the world.

"I don't much enjoy it," she sighed, dropping a ten thousand *yen* note into my begging bowl without batting an eye, "but I do get some pleasure out of doing it for him...."

Chapter Eight

He who fears that he shall suffer,
Already suffers what he fears.
Montaigne, 1580

A glistening morning after a night of rain. An enormous smiling sun, the color of Inca gold, peeping over a ridge line. The steep, dun-colored flank of a mountain, cut with jagged green gullies, curling lines of edible cactus, and ragged eucalyptus trees. A mud-walled farmhouse. A stone corral. The flash of water in an irrigation ditch. A *Quechua* boy. A barking dog. A flock of llamas. A white dirt road, dipping and coiling to accommodate the uneven, precipitous terrain. A cloud of dust. A caravan of pickup trucks. "GIFT OF THE AMERICAN PEOPLE" proclaimed the boxes they carried.

The trucks rounded a bend. Suddenly, the vast, flat, green carpet of the Amazon Basin appeared before them, ten thousand feet below and thirty miles away.

I was in the lead pickup truck, squeezed between two other Americans. On my right sat Greg Thwaite, the United States Vice-Consul for Cusco, a hefty, handsome Yale man, class of 1957. To my left was the driver, Billy Joe Hargis. Skinny and underdeveloped, with dirty blond hair, greasy skin, and a severe case of acne, Billy Joe looked and sounded like some kind of dust bowl survivor. In fact, he was a Peace Corps member, a recent graduate of Oklahoma A&M.

Greg had an air of superiority about him and did not condescend to talk much to us. But Billy Joe, wheeling the pickup truck around sharp mountain curves, down steep grades, had bent my ear ever since we left Cusco three days back, bragging about all his achievements, including the fact that he had distributed over fifty "Pigs for Peace" to the Quechua tribe of Cusco Province, helped them to build sanitary pig-pens, and instructed them on all the "do's and don'ts" of swine husbandry. Now they were all doing fine, he said; "the pigs, not the Injuns," for they stayed drunk on *chicha* beer most of the time, and "let their squaws do all the work."

Billy Joe and I had met four nights before at a café in the Plaza de Armas in Cusco. He was drinking Inca Cola. I was drinking shot after shot of Pisco, the local firewater, trying to explain to him why I had never been so scared in my life, despite my normal, inherited, love of feverish adventure.

My fear had a name: Hugo Blanco, "The Father of the Revolution." It had an occupation: leader of Marxist rebels. It even had a program: Inciting the Quechua peasants to revolt against their feudal white masters. In this province alone, according to the newspapers, seven haciendas had been "reformed" in the last three weeks. From what I'd heard, this "reformation" consisted of shooting any white man in sight, then handing the hacienda over to the Quechuas to be run as a commune.

"Where'd you get that shit?" scoffed Billy Joe when I brought it to his attention.

"It's common knowledge."

"Don't believe everything you hear."

"Now, don't get me wrong," I said. "I mean, I'm on the side of the Quechuas in this. The feudal land tenure system down here has got to go. It's not only unjust and sclerotic but..."

"Hey, you're gonna have to define that one for me, buddy-boy."

"It just doesn't make economic sense anymore."

"So, what's your problem?"

"I'll tell you my problem!" I erupted. "I just can't see getting my ass shot off for the mere fact that my skin pigment is a shade or two lighter than the locals. I mean, shit, I'm related to the little fuckers on one side."

"Hey, I'm part Cherokee myself," Billy Joe put in. "But hell, these are just isolated incidents. The government's got things in hand. And they've just come up with an idea that's gonna stop this thing from spreading."

"What's that?"

"They're sweeping the streets of every Injun of military age, drafting them into the army and putting them in special fenced camps where they can keep an eye on 'em."

"Oh, right!" I sneered. "That'll do the trick, won't it? Like jabbing a stick in a beehive."

"Simmer down now, feller," said Billy Joe. "I think you might just be in luck."

"Sure could use some . . ." I moaned.

"Yeah, there's an Alliance for Progress convoy leaving tomorrow for Puerto Carlos, down in the Amazon Basin."

"Jesus, why didn't you tell me that in the first place?"

"You didn't ask."

"How'd you hear about it?"

"I'm gonna be on it."

"Oh, you are a deep one, man," I sniffed. "Very deep."

"See," replied Billy Joe, chuckling at his own deviousness, "the trouble is all up here in the mountains. Down there in Puerto Carlos, they're all *mestizos*, not Injuns, and everything's *muy tranquilo*."

So, the next morning we got into six trucks, with twelve mestizo helpers, and set out for the Amazon Basin, handing out free food to the poor. As Vice Consul, Greg seemed particularly delighted to see the crowds of dark milling peasants—squat, long-skirted women in black derby hats, babies bundled on their backs, little hatchet-faced men in ponchos and skull caps—fighting to open those big grey AID boxes, each stamped with a brown hand and a white one clasped in a handshake.

Down, down we went into the lower valleys, out of the Altiplano, where the people were poorest, most restive.

Everyone had started to breathe a bit easier when the night before, in the town of Macapata, we learned that the insurrection had spread to several more provinces, including this one, and that it had even been called a *"Revolucíon"* by certain newspapers.

To relieve my growing signs of trepidation, which had perhaps affected even himself, Billy Joe assured me that within thirty-six hours we would be in Puerto Carlos, which was just "a hop, skip, and a jump from the Brazilian border."

Then—wouldn't you know it?—just hours from Puerto Carlos, when we could see the Amazon Basin spread out below us just a few miles away, out popped a band of little, bow-legged, barrel-chested, coca-chewing Quechuas in Cuban-style combat fatigues, each with an AK-47 in his hands.

At a signal from their leader, they filed out to block the roadway, raised their weapons, and leveled them at the lead pickup truck.

Billy Joe slammed on the brakes, as did the trucks behind us. Since there was nothing else that we could do, we all just sat there in the swirling white dust, waiting for something to happen.

Greg whispered his assurance that "nothing silly's going to happen because they've surely heard about all the good work we've been doing—giving out AID packages to the poor."

I shared so little of his optimism, however, that I could already feel warm liquid evidence to the contrary, pooling in my denim pants.

The leader of the band turned out to be young and tall for a Quechua, an intelligent fellow who spoke perfect English with—believe it or not—a soft, sweet, almost girlish Irish brogue. His face was remarkable for its dark, austere beauty, its large, expressive eyes, and there was something distinctly effeminate about the way he moved, despite his martial air. Like the others, he wore military fatigues and cradled an AK-47 in his arms. But he smiled brightly as he approached the cab of the pickup to invite us out for "a wee parley."

After we had walked down the road fifty meters, he motioned us to sit together under a small pepper tree that hung over the precipice.

"Sure now, it's a lovely day," the leader lisped, hovering over us like a schoolmistress. "Is it not, now?"

"Oh, yes sir, yes sir," we all agreed, it was a wonderful day.

"Say, where'd you learn such good English?" Billy Joe wanted to know.

"At the Catholic Action school in Cusco," said the leader, giggling. "Run by nuns from Dublin."

And we all had a laugh about that.

Removing the Cuban military cap from his head, he ran his long shapely fingers through his luxuriant hair and tossed his head prettily to get it out of his eyes.

Then, the leader pointed at the snow-covered mountains behind us to speak of their grandeur: "So high they seem quite unreal, do they not, now?" And he showed us something we hadn't noticed before, how each of the peaks was crowned with a ring of clouds, and how the clouds were of various shades, from deep black, almost purple, to frothy white, and how rare were the speckled patterns they made on the peaks.

Soon, a powerful wind swept down the mountain. Thunder sounded far off and drew nearer. Lightning zigzagged into the tops of the peaks. Then, in the leader's words, the circle round the peaks changed again, became a "great whirlwind of clouds, racing round the summits like mad dogs after their own tails."

"Wow!" marveled Billy Joe. "That sounds almost like poetry to me!"

But the leader appeared not to hear his words, and he said with a sweep of one long, slender, beautiful hand, "All this is *ours!*"

And we *gringos* all hastily agreed that yes, sir, it certainly did, it all belonged to the Peruvian people.

Then the leader asked us about our politics.

"I'm a Marxist-Leninist," I vehemently declared, "a dialectical materialist."

"I don't know much about politics," mumbled Billy Joe, "but I do believe in freedom for everybody."

Greg said he was a liberal Democrat, believed implicitly in the democratic process. He was about to quote Plato's Republic when the leader raised his hand to stop him.

"Aye," he said, "but there were slaves in that republic, as there are in this one."

BAM! BAM!

We all gasped when we heard gunfire back at the end of the column.

"Not to worry, lads," the leader chortled, playing up his accent.

"It's only me boys, havin' a wee bit of target practice."

Then the leader and I discovered that we had mutual literary interests. We both admired Garcia Lorca and Pablo Neruda.

Greg reminded us that at one time or another these men were all identified with the far left, "and that's fine, but one should always keep an open mind, let his reading range widely, be objective about the world."

"Perhaps," the leader retorted, "but under certain conditions, I believe, we must force ourselves to narrow our vision to achieve a specific goal. If we remain objective in the realm of politics and war, for instance, we will achieve nothing."

The leader flaunted his brilliant white teeth in a grin as he said this. We all grinned back and agreed that yes, under certain conditions that might be true.

Then a somber look appeared on his face.

"I must now tell you something," he sighed. "To be frank, gentlemen, you are in a bit of a pickle here. Me boys are all Quechuas from the Altiplano, beaten and starved by the white man since Pizarro landed over four hundred years ago. And they are out for blood."

"Blood?" I asked, swallowing bile.

"But after our wee parley here," the leader continued, smiling, ignoring my outburst, "I understand your point-of-view. And I have seen evidence of all the good works you've been doing, all up and down the road. So, I'd not like to see you at the mercy of 'me boys,' if you catch my meaning. For that reason, I'm afraid we shall have to go through a bit of a flimflam here."

"What... what kind of... flimflam?" I queried, my heart pounding in fear.

"I shall tell my men that I'll be managing the affair," the leader replied with a smirk. "I'll order them up the road, then I shall ask you all to go down on your knees beside the drainage ditch. I'll fire a shot into the mud. As I do, each of you in turn will fall forward to play dead till we've taken your lorries and gone."

"What . . . What about our helpers in the other trucks?" Greg wanted to know.

"They've been given a choice."

"What kind of choice?" I asked.

"Join us," said the leader, "or die."

"I fully understand," Greg put in, hastily. "And I'd like to take this opportunity to thank you, sir, for your kindness and consideration."

"Don't mention it," said the leader.

"Sir, one thing. If . . . If you don't mind me asking," I said.

"What's that, then?"

"Who . . . who *are* you?"

"Me?" he replied with a snicker. "I am 'the Mother of the Revolution.'"

"The . . . *what?*"

"Now, will you please march ahead of me?" he said, ignoring me, his voice full of irony. "I shall be pointing the gun at you, but not to worry, duckies. It's only a role we shall be playing, you see, an act to placate the Indians."

He stopped us briefly as we crossed over, calling out to his men in Quechua, ordering them up the road. Then he walked us single file to the edge of the ditch.

The three of us fell to our knees before him, side-by-side in the mud, facing the wall of the mountain.

I heard a shot, and Billy Joe fell forward, splashing face-first into the ditch.

Another shot and Greg did the same.

Waiting my turn, I could smell my own shit, and I knew I was going to die. Curiously, I thought of only one thing: my abandoned baby boy in California, whose name I would never know.

I heard the shot, fell into the ditch, and lay there for what seemed like forever, unsure of whether I was alive or dead.

"We . . . we can get up now," Greg assured us at last.

"You . . . You sure about that?" Billy Joel wanted to know.

"Yeah. They're gone."

"Where to?" I wondered aloud.

"Haven't a clue," Greg responded. "Into the ether, for all I know."

Later, I would wonder whether the "Mother of the Revolution" ever really existed at all.

Chapter Nine

*What we fear comes to pass
more speedily than what we hope.*
Publius Syrus, 1st Century B.C.

My next adventure was in Argentina, with an enormous, pale-eyed, raven-haired Patagonian of Welsh extraction named Maruja Rhys. A rumored diabolist and a certain nymphomaniac, she was employed as a typewriter technician at my place of work, an English language newspaper called the *Buenos Aires Herald*. There, she was known as *Maruja la Bruja*; or more prosaically in English, Maruja the Witch.

For no apparent reason, beyond the renowned olfactory magic of my clan, she conceived a passion for me on my first day of work. Then, much to the merriment of my colleagues, she continued to follow me about, staring moonily at me every day thereafter, inventing endless excuses to repair my Smith-Corona.

What my colleagues did not know (and I would die if they did) was that she lived directly above me in company housing on the Avenida Charcas, and every night she leaned out her window to throw worthless peso coins down onto my terrace, beckoning to me lasciviously when I came out to investigate.

For months, this went on. And she became more frenzied with her appeals, to the point where I feared that some inky night, she might tie her sheets together and, with her sooty mane flying like a Druidic handmaiden, slide down and attack me while I lay defenselessly in bed.

Then one evening, flush with too much wine, home from a lengthy, frustrating tangle with a comely Catholic colleague named Encarnacion Polnik, I threw myself down on my bed. Just as I was drifting off into an alcoholic stupor, Maruja la Bruja started tip-tip-tipping her coins on the tiles of my terrace again.

"*Ven paca, ven parriba!*" she beckoned, crooking a lustful finger at me when I stepped out on the terrace. "Come here, come up here!"

And I found myself weakening.

Creeping up the open stairway a few moments later, above the patio where my boss and his cronies played cards every night, dreading discovery, and the ridicule it would provoke at work, I cursed my family and their endless feverish affliction.

At which point, Maruja la Bruja flung open her door.

Naked as the night she was born, her vast, black, feathery V flaring nearly to her navel, she clamped onto my waist with a grip of iron, picked me up like a rag doll, bore me into her foul-smelling lair, fell backwards onto her rancid bed, and dragged me down on top of her.

Then, with a sigh that shook the rafters, she opened her arms, legs, and mouth to enfold me in a smothering embrace.

Instantly, I was sucked down, churned about, and spat out. In brief, she fucked like a teenage boy: Ravenous at first, she came in a second. Then, having gotten her way, she was no longer interested, and tossed me out on the landing like a pecked bone.

Not three minutes after I had crept up the stairs, I found myself slinking shamefully down them again, above the laughing men in the courtyard, who seemed to be pointing up at me.

For the next week, just as I feared, I was the butt of endless jokes at work, especially from that self-righteous Papist, Encarnacion Polnik. To make my humiliation complete, I found that everyone in the office was in on the joke, and that Encarnacion had put Maruja la Bruja up to the whole thing with hints that I reciprocated her feelings.

Even worse, Maruja had taken again to throwing coins down on my terrace.

So, one night, when the first officer of a Norwegian cargo ship walked into the sailor bar where I hung out in *La Boca* and announced that he was two men short and, sailing for Casablanca in the morning, I snapped up his offer.

I left *The Buenos Aires Herald* without giving notice, without a word of farewell to anyone in the office. I did not even collect my last week's salary.

And, at the risk of provoking Maruja la Bruja's necromantic ire, I must admit that I never regretted my decision for an instant....

Okay, all right... maybe for an hour or two, when she summoned a monstrous hurricane off the Cape Verde Islands to drive my ship onto a reef... maybe at that point, yes.

Chapter Ten

We are minor in everything but our passions.
ELIZABETH BOWEN, 1938

Back in the last century, near the village of Campello, in the province of Alicante, Spain, there existed a big, old, white-walled, tile-roofed hacienda perched on a sandy knoll above a beach. Known as "The Casa Campello," it was a kind of unconventional youth hostel that featured a communal kitchen, separate dorms for ladies and gents, a patio shaded by an immense date palm, and a clientele composed of young hitchhikers from all over Europe and North America. The *lingua franca* was English, the genders evenly divided, the girls tanned and healthy. There was a dense pine wood (convenient for liaisons, though fouled in places by toilet-less villagers) on the hill behind the house. The sea was warm, the guests free, easy and "down here for a good time."

"So, what's not to like?" I asked myself when I arrived penniless one autumn day, after a rough hitchhike from Gibraltar and a night on the beach.

Approaching Javier, the pot-bellied, avuncular Spaniard with a five o'clock shadow who ran the place, I frankly explained my plight. He heard me out, expressed admiration for my adventurous spirit, and made the following proposal: I would work for him eight hours a day, at any task he might choose for my room and board. There would be no cash exchange at all.

With my stomach rumbling, I agreed with alacrity, then went to work cleaning toilets right after lunch. For a week or two, he doled out only the worst jobs to me, but I labored without protest, always doing my best. He appreciated my effort, and when his Dutch bartender suddenly quit, he offered me the job.

The first of many good things about the job was that the barmaid and I could keep all our tips, so now I had spending money. Second was that I worked nights, so I could spend my days on the beach, swimming, working on my tan, and chatting up the girls. Third was that the barmaid was Carol Popplewell, a shapely, young English girl from Bexleyheath, Kent, whom I had been eyeing since my arrival. It was she, in fact, who had awakened me on the beach, pointing me up the hill toward the Casa Campello on my first morning in town. Unfortunately, she had a male companion named "Bean," who had been her bosom friend since grammar school, and they appeared to be inseparable.

A week after I started at the cantina, Bean had to go back to work on the London Underground. He and Carol had a tearful parting in the patio after breakfast with the whole Casa watching. Everyone seemed moved by their emotion, but I could not wait to see the last of the bastard.

"Silly git, old Bean," Carol said laughing, a few days after he had departed. "He warned me against you. So, of course you were the first thing I thought of, Ernesto, the minute he left."

I liked Carol very much indeed. At first, I liked her simply for the way she operated in the bar, effortlessly calm, graceful, soft-spoken, no matter how rude or rowdy the customers might be. I thought she was just super cool and collected, but later I found that she, like most of us at the Casa, was stoned most of the time.

There was a bit of South London in her voice, a tendency to drop her double t's, but not thank God her aitches, for she had worked hard on her accent. What came across was something hip, classless, big city: sophistication without any particular "breeding."

Working behind the bar at night, hanging out at the beach all day, showing off my handsome young face and suntanned pecs, I had plenty of time to observe Carol. And observe her I did, from head to toe.

She wore her hair long. Chestnut in color, it was streaked lighter in places from the sun. While at work, she had the delightful, seductive habit of flicking it to the right, to get it out of her face. At the beach, she pinned it up like a Victorian lady, showing off her long, elegant neck.

Her forehead was high, Anglo-Saxon, her brows plucked in thin, up-slanting line. Her eyes? Large, heavily-lidded, with long lashes—their color a deep blue/grey, like the North

Atlantic in summer. Her nose? High-bridged, straight, with a little downward curve at the tip. Her lips? Full, and so red that she toned them down with light, pinkish lipstick.

For someone with such natural grace, such self-confidence, Carol smiled rarely, a bit shyly, which only added to her allure. When she did crack a grin, the contrast of her perfectly white un-British teeth against the deep golden tan of her face was spectacular. Her laugh was rare, but well worth waiting for. Low, rather delicate, it lit her beautiful countenance with an infinitely seductive light ... at least from my biased point of view.

And her body in a bikini? Only my master, James Joyce, could do it justice: "*Dimber wapping dell-pretty wench ...*"

What I liked most about Carol, even more than her overtly sexual attributes, was her long, slender, elegant fingers that I watched every night when she carried her tray to the bar. When she used them to gesture or make a point, they were as graceful as a ballerina's.

After her Bean boy left, I approached her slowly, feeling my way along. Cleaning the bar with her after closing time, I had plenty of time to get to know her. What I learned, I liked even more.

Her father worked for the Post Office. Her mother was a housewife. She was a war baby, the child of an unmarried English girl and a Canadian flyer adopted by the childless Popplewells in 1944. Her parents were relentlessly working class. When she was a child, they restricted her reading because she might "damage" her eyes. Later, when she bought some pretty bauble, they would say, "Why waste your money on that, then? It ain't for our class, is it?"

Carol refused to let them browbeat her, even though they made her quit school at sixteen and go to work as a shop girl in Bexleyheath High Street. She made it a point to visit the public library four nights a week. There, she went about systematically educating herself, creating herself, discovering literature, history, painting, even music, all on her own.

I loved the way she told her story, slowly, calmly, over a late-night cigarette and a cognac after the bar closed, and I found myself falling for her, disquietingly, feverishly so. In a way, I was almost glad that Bean had so recently departed, for out of discretion, I had to resist declaring my intentions.

Instead, I told Carol my life story, including the tale of my infamous clan, leaving nothing out. Taking my cue from Camus, "*A man defines himself by his make-believe as well as by his sincere impulses,*" I exaggerated my family's outrageous sexual shenanigans. And I was encouraged that she displayed no shock or dismay, that on the contrary she found my tales "rather titillating, Ernesto."

I loved the way she pronounced my name, in the English manner, with the silent "r" in the middle; and I equally adored the slightly mocking tone she took with me, a tone that women sometimes employ on men to whom they are attracted.

Then one night after work, ten days after Bean left town, Carol took my hand without a word and walked me down to the beach. We sat together in the sand, hand in hand, for the longest time, gazing up at the stars, saying nothing, until she dropped her head on my shoulder. I put an arm about her slender waist, then squeezed her to me, marveling at how soft she was, how her body gave against mine. We fell backward on the sand, and instantly we were sucking the life out of each other.

We fell asleep in the sand, awakening only when the sun rose up out of the Mediterranean. We strolled back to the Casa arm in arm, just in time for breakfast. Although everyone immediately noticed our new relationship, and I saw a couple of eyebrows raised, no one said a word about us. A permissive atmosphere prevailed at the Casa Campello: *menages a trois*, public fornication, sexual dramas of every kind were commonplace.

Carol and I packed a lunch together and later that morning hiked to a secret cove we knew. There, we just lay in the sand all day, under a little acacia tree, falling asleep now and then, saying little of importance, relying on what we could see written in the other's eyes. Her skin smelled of salt and sea air. Her body was warm to the touch.

In the late afternoon, after a swim out to sea, I got her to read to me from a little volume of Jacques Prevert's poetry that she had carried with her.

She chose a poem entitled *"Alicante,"* which happened to be the name of a town nearby:

> *Une orange sur la table*
> *Ta robe sur le tapis*
> *Et toi dans mon lit*

Doux présent du présent
Fraîcheur de la nuit
Chaleur de ma vie

An orange on the table
Your dress on the rug
And you in my bed
Sweet present of the present
Freshness of the night
Warmth of my life

Her voice was clear and cool when she read, her pronunciation of French *parfait*.

"That is so beautiful!" I said. "But where'd you learn such good French?"

"In France, of course, you silly git. I was an *au pair* in Paris for a year and a half, wasn't I?"

"What else is there that I don't know about you?"

"More than you could ever imagine," she replied, laughing, nudging me in the ribs.

We were hip to hip in our swimsuits, near naked, the sun hot on our bodies. Her skin so brown, her belly so round, her breasts so . . .

"I love you," I whispered.

But Carol just smiled, gazed at me with her afternoon eyes, and went back to reading.

On our way back to the Casa Campello that evening, with the sun going down behind the Sierra de Abanilla, we spoke of colors.

"You are red. That's clear, isn't it?" Carol said of me. "And I'm blue, yah?"

"Exactly," I replied. "We're like fire and water. And what I'd like to do right now is just . . . drown in you."

"Don't speak so quickly, Ernesto, you might just get your wish."

Next day at the beach, I constructed a little sand house.

"If it falls down," I said, "that means we're not going to make it, but if it stays up even against the tide that means we'll be together always."

When the tide started coming in, and it looked like the house might fall, Carol set to work helping me, and it stood up against everything the sea threw at it. She made a wall, a garden, a path, and a terrace for the sun. Then she broke off two little sticks and said, very softly, "This is you; this is me."

I looked at her in a certain way, and she said, "Oh, right!" She broke off another smaller stick and said, "This is a half-grown one."

Then she got a tiny, tiny stick, placing it next to the other three. "This is the baby," she murmured, and I thought I would die of joy.

"Yes," she went on, rapturously, "there shall be a whole great brood of them running wild under the redwood trees in California. I can just see them now!"

On the way home to the Casa that afternoon, Carol stopped abruptly, with her hands full of beach things, looked me in the eye, and said, "The thing is, Ernesto, it's all a bit of a lark, isn't it?"

"What?"

"I don't think I'm the kind of girl you imagine at all. Not really the sticking sort, you see. More fun with just a random pick-up than a steady bloke. After all, I'm only twenty-one years old. You are so bloody sincere, Ernesto, when what I really crave sometimes is just a good shag. Know what I mean?"

"You trying to warn me?" I asked. "Or what?"

"Yes, I should think I am," she replied, putting on a posh accent. Then she lit up with a smile. "But don't let that put you off, old egg."

Monday was our night off, so we hitched into Alicante to find a room, some place to be alone. We looked everywhere, but they didn't want guests if they weren't married. This was the time of Franco: *Opus Dei* and the Spanish Catholic Church were ascendant; rules against "immorality" were strictly enforced. On the verge of giving up, we tried one last *pensión*, and with a little bribe, they let us in!

Our room was on the roof, with potted plants and a view of the harbor. Plain but clean, with a squeaky double bed, it seemed fine to us. We went out to dinner at a little workingman's restaurant around the corner where we loaded up on *pescado, patatas fritas* and dry white wine. On the way home, we popped some of Carol's Benzedrine pills.

She looked so pretty in her pink sleeveless mini frock that I almost hated to remove it, but I unzipped it down the back as soon as we got in the door. Off with her bra and bikini panties in a flash. This was the first time I'd had a chance to see all of her, in full electric light, and what I saw pleased me infinitely.

We fell to bed, and she murmured the words I had been dying to hear.

"I love you," she said, as she opened her legs to me. "I really love you, don't I?" she said again, as if astonished by the notion, when I came inside.

And what was it like?

"*Honeysauces*" said the master, "*sugar of roses, marchpane, gooseberried pigeons, ringocandies...*"

Yet, for the next week, we had little peace, bickering on the job like an old married couple. The intensity of our feelings for each other frightened us because it signified the end of youth, and freedom, the beginning of responsibility.

Then one night a tall, handsome Jamaican with a head full of natty dreads came strutting into the bar. A drug dealer named Rupert, he had once known Carol and Bean casually in London. He asked her to a late-night party at his beach house, and she accepted gladly, though I was pointedly excluded.

She did not get in the next morning until 9 a.m. I knew because I was sitting under the date palm tree sipping my coffee when she arrived, looking a bit used up.

"Have fun?" I asked.

"Yes," she said, "but I couldn't bear to see him today. Just too bloody intense. Will you come with me to the beach?"

"For protection?"

"If you like," she replied, and we had a wonderful time all day long, laughing, playing in the waves, avoiding all unpleasant topics.

Days occur like this, sometimes illogically, gifts of brief rainfall in a dry land.

We decided to go back to our *pensión* in Alicante after work. There, we made love all night again. With the aid of Benzedrine, it was even better than the first time.

In the morning, though, Carol said, "I shall be off now, love. He's leaving for Paris in a day or two. I should like to spend some time with him before he goes. But don't get all soggy on me, yah? My feelings for you have nothing to do with him. You see, I can fancy you and fancy him at the same time."

"How do you feel about him, exactly?"

"Oh, he's nil. Nothing to him, really. Just a bit of chocolate lolly. Won't last a moment. And you're this great lovely organic peach, aren't you? But that's not going to stop me. It's me nature, i'n'it?"

"Oh, yes, it is, Carol," I observed, bitterly. "I'm quite familiar with it. It's what I've been trying to avoid all my life."

She disappeared the next day, without giving notice. People at the Casa said she'd run off with Rupert in his Jaguar.

I had come halfway 'round the world to be paid in my own coin. Or as Malraux put it: *"A certain depth of misery is like the thought of death: it puts human beings in their proper places."*

Some years later, when I was in graduate school at San Francisco State, I was surprised to receive a note from Carol, forwarded by my mother in Southern California: "I'm in New York, love, heading out to California by bus, and I should be frightfully grateful if I might kip at your flat for a fortnight's time. What do you say?"

Having just more or less amicably ended a relationship with a young fashion model, I found myself free for the moment, and I must admit that the old excitement came over me when I read her letter.

Yet, which of us does not fear disappointment in the rekindling of old flames?

When I drove down to pick Carol up at the Greyhound bus station, I almost walked right past her. She had put on a little weight. Not that she was fat. She was still just as beautiful as ever, but no longer my Spanish waif. She was a woman of twenty-seven years, and she looked every minute of it.

In the car, on the way to my apartment, Carol chirped away a bit nervously, awkwardly, unsure of herself, trying to please. Her South London accent, which I had once adored, grated a bit upon my ears which were now attuned to the hipper, cooler tones of the Haight-Ashbury District where I lived.

A few years before, Carol had the power of life and death over me: *"You turned me into your pet piggy, rooting around in the refuse at the peripheries of your consciousness,"* I wrote in my journal of the time. Now here she was, this chatty, dolly London bird bending my ear.

We made love as soon as we got home, as if to put that part behind us. And though it was still good, it was not Spain—not Spain by a long shot.

That night at dinner, Carol seemed brighter, more self-confident. The old fire came back, and she started spinning me tales the way she used to, making me laugh over her trials and turmoil of the past few years.

She had been everywhere, it seemed, done everything, had every man she wanted, and more.

Rupert had not lasted a month.

"Well, you still look great," I remarked, "whatever you've been through."

"Yes," she said, acknowledging the compliment with a small self-deprecating grin. "But inside I'm a bit done in, you see. Tired of all the craziness and drugs."

"What are you looking for now?"

"I'm looking," she replied, with something of the old rakish smile, "for a little house under the redwood trees, and a brood of kiddies running wild and naked in the woods."

"Sorry, Carol," I said, frowning, shaking my head, "but I'm afraid it's too late for that now."

Yet, for the next few days we had a wonderful time together, reminiscing about our mad youth in Spain; and the old flame flickered up for a time, before finally dying out.

That was not the end of it (we lingered together through August, September, October of that year), but it might as well have been.

When Pilar, an old girlfriend of mine from the United Farmworkers Union, showed up one night with her biker husband, looking for a place to stay, she slept with Carol and me in my double bed while big Chato kipped on the narrow couch in my front room.

In the middle of the night, I heard Pilar whispering in my ear, *"Oye, Ernesto, tu novia es razonable, liberal?* Your girlfriend, is she open-minded?"

"Completamente," I whispered back. "What about your husband?"

"Are you serious? He's Mexican! But thank God he sleeps like the dead."

She pulled up her CHICANO POWER T-shirt, exposing her spectacular bronze breasts, then mounted me like an Aztec goddess, huffing and puffing, making little, inadvertent, squeaking noises. At one point, it got so wild that we rolled out of bed, hitting the floor with a bang, and I feared that the *bandido* in the next room would come running in to cut out my heart, but he slept through it all, blissfully unaware.

Carol, on the other hand, merely pretended to slumber. When Pilar and I had reached and surpassed the pinnacle of our exertions, had crawled back in bed, and were lying beside Carol, I reached over to pat her on the thigh, where I found her wet with desire.

Inspired, I grabbed Pilar's right hand with my left and guided it over my lower body to Carol's hot prickly cauldron, where my right hand had been busy stirring up a bubbling froth. Instantly, both ladies caught their breath. For a moment, I was afraid that Carol would balk, but she settled into the slower, lighter, more knowledgeable female rhythm of Pilar's circling fingers very quickly, leaving me free to explore other options.

Ten minutes later the three of us were at it again, in a new, unusual way.

Yet, when we awakened in the morning, we avoided one another's eyes, as if the light of dawn had filled us with some residual sense of indignity.

Feeling a need to diffuse the tension, I tried a joke: "I tell you, ladies, there's only one thing I regret about last night."

"What's that?" Pilar wanted to know.

"That I don't have two pricks," I replied, but neither lady laughed.

With the dirty stuff, Carol and I had given up on love, and we never mentioned the word again.

I had no idea how this had affected her until one night I came home from class to find her sitting naked on my bed, plucking out her pubic hair one by one. There was a little pile of them on the sheet beside her, and the left side of her pubis was bald.

It was some kind of message, I supposed, but pretended not to notice, and left the room.

In November, when offered a job as nanny to a rock impresario's kids in Aspen, Colorado, with free skiing thrown in, Carol accepted.

A week later, I wrote her a letter, just to say hello. She wrote back, just to let me know that she was getting on fine.

That was the last we knew of each other until eleven years later.

I was a successful writer by then, with two best-selling novels to my credit, and I owned a home in Hampstead, an upscale neighborhood in London. It was Christmas Eve, and I had just walked into the Knightsbridge tube station with my arms full of gifts for my wife and daughter when, by an incredible twist of fate, I witnessed an altercation that I was never, ever, meant to see.

Carol had just been arrested by a pair of London bobbies. At first, I thought they had caught her trying to sneak into the tube without paying, a common enough offense, one of which even I had been guilty. It quickly became apparent, however, that they suspected Carol of having shoplifted expensive merchandise from Harrods' department store. They were trying to lead her off peaceably for interrogation, without clapping the cuffs on her, but she was resisting, protesting indignantly:

"'Ow dare you? Take yer bleedin' 'ands off me this instant!"

Carol was dressed presentably enough in a shop lady's long, open woolen coat, with a clean but frayed white blouse, a well-worn tweed skirt and run-down high heels. And despite the visible lines about her mouth and eyes, she was at thirty-eight still slender and attractive.

Yet, in her agitation and distress, she had let her accent drop to a closer approximation of her antecedents than she would have liked. Whatever the case, it was evident to even the most casual observer that she was guilty as hell. It showed all over her face.

My heart flew out to Carol then, but I stood rooted in my tracks for one of the longest moments of my life, attempting to assimilate what my boggled eyes told me to be true, while busy commuters, arms full of bags and boxes, bumped and weaved around me, uttering little harrumphs of irritation.

I desperately attempted to formulate a course of action, but the fact was that I was torn between two warring impulses. One was to simply march up to the police and vouch for Carol, attesting to her character as an old friend, alluding to a mental trial that she was going through. The other was to get the fuck out of there before she caught sight of me in this moment of her most profound humiliation. I hesitated too long though, and what I most dreaded happened.

Carol saw me.

Her eyes that I remembered so well, so deep, so Atlantic blue, went wide, then a kind of veil fell over them.

Her head dropped.

Her body went slack, and she delivered herself into the hands of the coppers without a whimper.

Chapter Eleven

It is vain to find fault with those arts of deceiving wherein men find pleasure to be deceived.
JOHN LOCKE, 1690

Three weeks after I left the Casa Campello, I found myself in Rome with nary a lira to my name. Camping in the Stazione Termini with other assorted vagabonds, stashing my backpack in a jimmied locker, I began to feel the first unmistakable symptoms of 'nefarious fever,' that virulent subspecies of 'mendacious fever'.

One afternoon, dressed as presentably as possible under the circumstances, I was strolling across the Piazza Navona when I fixed my attention upon a thin, pink-cheeked young fellow with balding blond hair, bulbous yet furtive blue eyes, and a sparse, neatly trimmed moustache. Seated on a bootblack perch, he was trying without much success to make conversation with the elderly Italian seated beside him. To go native, perhaps, he had adorned a shiny black jacket and boots of beautiful Italian leather. Yet, there was an impatient, distracted innocence about him that could only be American. Though he wore no clerical collar, he looked as if he might have. All of which indicated to me, based on much experience, that he might be an easy mark.

I approached him with hopes of simply hitting him up for five hundred lire or so, but he turned out to be the talkative sort. Even before I got a chance to ask him for money, he had introduced himself, invited me for lunch in a nearby café, and was telling me the story of his life.

His name was Tim O'Malley. A fellow Californian, he was raised in San Francisco and went to Harvard, where he studied architecture. After college, he traveled to Geneva for work in the atelier of a celebrated protege of Le Corbusier. There he met a beautiful French girl, also an architectural student, named Danielle de Montigny. He married her, brought her back to the States, and they settled in San Francisco.

Though trained as an architect, Tim found it more interesting to start his career as a builder. What he loved, he said, was buying up beautiful, old, San Francisco Victorian houses, renovating them, then selling them for a profit. Business was good, and everything went fine for a couple of years until his best friend and former college roommate, Marc-Antonio Trivulzio, the black sheep of a rich, aristocratic, Neapolitan family, fell upon hard times and came to stay with them in Pacific Heights.

Tim was out of the house twelve to fifteen hours a day. Marco and Danielle had time on their hands, and they did lots of drugs. They were both exceptionally good looking, and so utterly "Euro" in mentality that Tim often felt excluded from their conversations. It was no big surprise, therefore, when he came home one afternoon and caught them in bed.

"Sleeping like babies, they were," he sniffed.

Being the understanding sort, Tim crept out of the room, left them in peace, and only confronted them with their indiscretion when he returned that evening. After listening to their apologies, their excuses (they blamed it on cocaine), their vows that it would never happen again, he agreed to let bygones be bygones on the condition that Marco leave the house immediately, and that any further intercourse between them be conducted solely by mail. Considering their passionate, Latin temperaments, the lovers put up only the briefest argument. Marco left the house and Tim had another month of domestic bliss before coming home one night to find Danielle gone.

Acting on a "strong hunch," he said, he checked his financial status the next morning to find his second largest bank account looted in its entirety.

"I've come for them here because I know them both very well," he told me. "Europe is the only place where they can be happy."

"Have you checked with their families?" I enquired.

"Yes, and neither of them know a thing."

"What are you going to do when you find them?"

"I might be naïve," he replied, shaking his head, "but I'm going to persuade Danielle to come back to me, and try to get back some of the money. It was quite a substantial amount."

"Tell you what," I said, thinking fast. "I used to be in law enforcement in the States, and I might be able to help you find them. I wouldn't charge you anything near what you'd have to pay a private detective over here."

Tim looked interested. After a few drinks, after he had described the lovers to me in detail, we agreed on a price that seemed, at this particularly embarrassing point in my life, quite a princely sum.

"Half up front," said Tim. "The other half on delivery."

"Deal," I replied, nodding. "With one condition. If I find them within ten days, I get a twenty percent bonus."

We shook hands, Tim hit me with the agreed-on sum, I gave him my California driver's license as security, and I was on my way.

One of the things I found on the road is that coincidence is the norm, while chance is but a common denominator: Though I didn't feel obliged to divulge the information to Tim, I knew right where I was going. To tell the truth, I knew exactly where the errant lovers were hiding. They had rented a discreet, cliffside villa in the beautiful, fashionable, rather artsy village of Positano, on the Amalfi Coast not far from Naples. I had seen them on the beach there several times, when I stopped for a bit of R & R after an arduous, perilous hitchhike around Sicily, and a harrowing ferry-ride across the Straits of Charybdis (another story).

They were a remarkable-looking couple. Once you'd laid eyes on them, you could not possibly forget them.

Marco was tall and gaunt, with a long narrow skull, pale skin, and thin, sandy hair that hung over his brow. He looked more English than Italian, like some kind of egghead intellectual. Although Tim, quoting the Irish master we both held in esteem, claimed that he *"hadn't a groatsworth of wit."*

Danielle was tall, dark-skinned, and voluptuous. Seemed more Italian than French. She was of *Pied Noir* origin, like the film star Claudia Cardinale, to whom she bore an uncanny resemblance.

Unlike her partner in crime, she was not without talent or intelligence, but it had "all gone to shit with drugs," according to her spouse.

So, I rode the train down to Naples, got a bus to Positano, established that the wayward duo were still ensconced in their secret love nest, checked myself into a little *pensione* above the cove, and spent the next week or so vacationing on Tim's generosity.

I waited in Positano not only because I wanted Tim to think he was getting his money's worth, and I happened to be enjoying myself immensely, but also because I had deduced something important about his character. There was in his awkward, self-conscious manner, in his damp, evasive yet protuberant blue eyes, in his Irish-Catholic background, his past as an altar boy, a strong indication that on some level he was enjoying all the torment, that he had perhaps been its principal instigator.

Ten days after our last meeting, I collected Tim at the Naples railway station and hired a taxi to Positano. I pointed out the lovers' pink villa on its cliff above the turquoise sea, its walls adorned with jasmine, its garden with rose trees. Then I awaited him, impatiently, on the beach at the bottom of their steep flagstone stairway, while he conducted his lengthy business.

Pacing up and down the pebbly strand, going over all possible scenarios, I began to feel a bit antsy. I'd thought I had Tim figured, but he was not an easy man to read. One thing I did know about him for sure: There was a wholly different person, quite another cup of tea indeed, which simmered just below the surface of his consciousness, never quite coming to a boil. Who that person was . . . nobody knew.

Not even Tim himself.

"What if he takes it into his head to murder them?" I asked myself. "Does that make me an accessory to the crime?"

Just when my paranoia had reached its apex, and I was on the verge of clambering up the precipitous cobbled streets for the taxi stand, Tim stepped casually down the stairs to meet me, stopping to sniff the jasmine and admire the view of Capri.

"She's agreed to give it another try," he said, without visible emotion, handing over my driver's license and the balance of my fee in a plain brown envelope. "We'll try a month's holiday in Porto Santo Stefano, see what transpires."

"Great," I said, smothering a sigh of relief. "But what if it doesn't work out?"

"Then she's free to do as she likes," he blandly replied.

I stayed in Positano, renting one of the picturesque (but damp and slug-ridden) little cave houses dug into the side of the cliff, fairly sure that I had not seen the last of old Tim.

When Marco suddenly disappeared from the scene, my suspicions increased. A week later, when Tim showed up with a further tale of woe, they were but confirmed. Danielle, with

Marco's probable collusion, had bilked him of another several thousand dollars and disappeared again.

"All right," I sighed, with the forbearance of a man who had everything to gain and nothing to lose. "What do you want now, Tim?"

"I want to find her again."

"You still want her back?"

"No," he said. "All I want is my money."

"Let me tell you something, man. She is not going to give it up unless you get the law onto her. And it would be hard to prove. She's your wife, after all, theoretically entitled to half your assets."

"What do you suggest?"

"You say this Marco guy is from a rich, aristocratic family?"

"Absolutely," Tim said. "One of the oldest and richest in Naples. They can trace their roots right back to Pompeii."

"Well, I suggest that you get a lawyer then," I advised. "Approach the family, tell them the story, ask them to reimburse you. After all, they know you already. You were his college roommate! They have no reason to distrust your word. Plus, I'm sure that by now they're used to Marco's imbroglios. But if they do refuse, for some reason, you just tell them you'll sue them, publicize it all over Italy, bring shame on their family name. These old, aristocratic, Neapolitan Catholic families are proud of their reputations. It might just do the trick."

"Brilliant. When do we start?"

"We?"

"Sure," said Tim. "I'm going to need your advice and counsel on this. You speak some Italian. You've been right on everything up to now. I trust your judgment, and I'm willing to pay for it."

"I'll want at least twenty percent of everything you get," I insisted.

"You're on," he said, smiling, nodding enthusiastically.

So, we rented a car, drove to Naples, acquired a high-priced Italian lawyer, then met with the family in the courtyard garden of their vast old mansion on the Via Santa Brigida.

The father, Michele, was a tall, elegant, rather fey-looking, old gentleman in a tan summer suit and a broad straw hat. The mother, Giulia, though considerably younger, was immensely fat, wearing a dark silk dress that revealed far more of her than anyone might ever desire to see. The daughter, Fausta, on the other hand, was a beautiful eighteen-year-old in tennis clothes, for whom I instantly fell, as they say in Italy, "like a ton of pasta."

Nevertheless, I remained firm on Tim's behalf.

When the father protested that he had washed his hands of his prodigal son, that he'd disowned him, written him out of his will, I threatened to initiate a lawsuit. Not only that, but I would phone every major newspaper in Naples to publicize all of Marco's transgressions, including embezzlement, drug use, alienation of affections, and cohabitation, which was still a crime in Italy. After our lawyer produced documents to prove most of our allegations, including love letters, bank statements, and a copy of the rental contract for the villa in Positano, the family caved in without further protest, summoned their banker, and within a week Tim and I were "sitting pretty" again.

Just before we left our hotel in Naples, Tim got a phone call from the island of Corfu. It was his wife and his former best friend.

First Danielle got on the phone, hinting that they might be able to get back together again. I watched Tim carefully as he took her call, and when he looked in danger of relenting, when he got a puny, weepy look in his eye, and his thin, reddish, lower lip started to quiver, I elbowed him in the ribs and shook my head vehemently, mouthing the words, "Be a mensch!"

"I'm sorry, Danielle," he said, mustering his courage.

"Come on, Tim," she replied, "who are you kidding? We all know this is how you get off. You ought to be paying us."

When that did not get a rise out of him either, Marco grabbed the phone.

"A gentleman," he said, in a sternly admonitory tone—"*un gentiluomo*"—does not bring families into these matters."

"Well, Marco, I guess I'm just not a gentleman, then," Tim retorted, and I was almost proud of him when he hung up.

He paid me off again, we said goodbye, he caught a plane for San Francisco, and I never expected to see him again.

I stayed on in Naples after Tim left, enjoying a degree of financial security which had hitherto been quite unknown to me.

Naples in the sixties was so cheap that for a mere pittance, by American standards, I could live the life of a wealthy man-about-town, a life to which I rapidly became accustomed.

Following Tim's example, I bought myself some beautiful Italian boots and got a tailor on the Corso Umberto Uno to measure me for a fine suit of clothes. For seventy dollars a month, I rented a furnished luxury apartment in the Borgo Marinaro with a roof garden and a view of Vesuvius and the Bay of Naples. For another sixty dollars a month, I hired a pretty housekeeper named Maria, a married woman with a home and family of her own, who occasionally and obligingly doubled as my siesta-mate.

I slept late every morning and went out to restaurants, bars, theaters, concerts, and coffee houses until late every night. With my rapidly improving Italian, and the Neapolitan people's inherent warmth and geniality, it was not long before I had established casual relationships with several of the local dandies and artistic folk who hung out near the Palazzo Reale. And within no time, it seemed, I was being invited out to dinner parties nearly every night.

Naples at that time had only a few young resident foreigners and a tiny monied class. So, it was not long before I was introduced, according to my intentions, to the marvelous Fausta Trivulzio, sister to the scoundrel Marc-Antonio Trivulzio.

"May I present my American friend, Signor Ernesto Brawley?" said Carlo Monte, an acquaintance from Via Toledo, at a party one night at the mansion of a purported *Camorra* (Mafia) don.

"Signor Brawley and I are already acquainted," Fausta coolly replied. "And it is my sincere desire that I never lay eyes on him again."

Yet, there was something in the girl's bright, green eyes that set me to wondering. Was it amusement? Mockery?

Later that night, emboldened by gross infusions of Sambucca Romana, I asked her to dance. And I was not completely surprised when she raised her eyebrows for only a second before turning into my arms.

"What a coincidence that we should meet here, Signor Brawley," she sneered, "on this festive occasion, after what you and your friend have done to my—"

"Ah, but it is no coincidence!"

"No?"

"Absolutely no!"

"Then, pray, *signore*," she said, "tell me what it is, *per favore*."

"*É destino!*" I cried out, with all the fervor in my lying heart.

And when Fausta laughed despite herself, an infectious burbling laugh that lit up her little round face, I knew I was already halfway there.

It took a while, but after running into Fausta a few more times in the social swirl of Naples, I began to detect a rebel in her. She had something of her brother's adventurous spirit, without his selfishness or venality.

She liked that I was a wanderer and that Naples was but a way-stop on my odyssey around the world backwards.

"Oh, if only I were a man, I should do likewise!" she gushed, in her schoolgirl's British English. "I should travel the world from end to end . . . backwards!"

"You don't have to be a man," I responded. "You've just got to have one along for the ride."

"And you are proposing yourself for the role of my protector?"

"And why not?"

"Has it never occurred to you that since you are my enemy," Fausta growled, "and the enemy of my family, you might not be the ideal candidate for my affections?"

"Have you never read Romeo and Juliet?" I asked, and she fell into my arms with laughter.

Fausta studied at the *Istituto del'Arte,* on Corso Malta. She would never be a great artist, like the local, Artemisia Gentileschi, but her charcoal drawings were witty and precise, and the one she did of me was a bit too good for comfort, capturing as it did—and even subtly exaggerating—my squinty eyes.

Yet, paradoxically, it was then, upon discovering her talent for perversity, that I fell into her pink, little palms like a feather ripe for plucking.

At first sight, Fausta did not look like anybody's idea of an aristocrat. She was neither tall nor thin. Her posture was neither stiff nor particularly erect. Her face was not severe. Her cheekbones were not high. She had no Hapsburg jaw or eagle beak. Instead, at eighteen, her honey-colored hair was fine as an infant's. Her lips and cheeks were puffy and pink. Her arms, breasts, hips, tummy, and thighs were still plump with baby fat. I called her beautiful, but that was only my own highly subjective opinion. In fact, the casual observer might prefer the term "Renoir-like" to describe Fausta, and go on to say, "She's got the kind of looks that don't last."

A more elegant way to put it might be Beaudelaire's: *"La beauté, c'est l'infini dans le fini."*

A cherry blossom beauty, as the Japanese said: sweet, ripe, and infinitely precious for the very fact that it was ephemeral.

Which only made my fever for her flame higher.

Oddly enough, Fausta's ne'er-do-well brother, Marco, presented me with the opportunity I had been waiting for. He appeared in the marketplace in the Piazza Santo Domenico Maggiore one morning, dead ass broke and utterly alone.

"Hey, man," he said, in the stoners' English that was the international *lingua franca* of the time. "What's up? Haven't seen you since Positano. Aren't you a friend of Tim's?"

"Uh, maybe, yeah," I replied warily.

Yet, in the ensuing conversation he displayed no indignation for my role in his downfall, or even for Tim's, but saved it all for Danielle.

"The bitch abandoned me without a *centisimo*. But where would she be without me? She owes me, don't you think?"

"No question," I said, for what would it gain me to quarrel?

Marco seemed so pathetically grateful for the support of his erstwhile enemy that I was inspired to add, "But hey, listen, man, if you need a few *lire* to cop . . ."

In short, all it took was a small *dono*, a bribe, to feed his habit, and Fausta's bro was now my bosom buddy.

Soon, I even had him running notes between his sis and me, setting up rendezvous at my apartment, then discreetly departing when we wanted to be alone.

"In a world where Lot pimped his own daughters to the Sodomites," I scribbled in my journal, *"what are your sins in comparison, Marco?"*

Fausta would not make love with me. Not until, as she said, "we are on our way round the world backwards together."

Yet, each small kiss from her rosebud lips burnt like fire.

Even so, I did nothing to rush her. For the first time in my life, I desired someone for herself, not for what she could give me. I liked the feeling of being responsible for someone. Fausta was so childlike, so unworldly, I wanted to take care of her. The idea of removing her tennis clothes, picking her up and setting her into a tub of water, soaping her down and running a washcloth over her, lifting her out of the tub, and drying her off, wrapping a white towel around her soft, roseate skin, was my kind of heaven.

We started making plans for our departure. It had to be done in secret because Fausta's family cloistered her like a nun, she said, and they already had an effete Neapolitan aristocrat, a "closet queen," as she called him, picked out for her as a husband. Fausta needed money, she said, to bribe her brother and the servants, to buy clothes for the journey, to pay off certain debts that she owed. . . .

The money mounted up, higher and higher, until it started to hurt, and I finally began to have my suspicions. I did not mention them to Fausta. Indeed, I tried to conceal them from myself. But perhaps she saw the disappointment in my eyes, or she heard it in my voice.

So, she moved up the night of our departure.

"Let us do it now! I cannot wait to be alone with you," she whispered passionately into my ear in the secluded cafe where we met in Posillipo.

That night she arranged for the rear gate and the inner doors to the Trivulzio mansion to remain unlocked. I sneaked inside at precisely 2:00 a.m. according to Fausta's instructions and made my way up through the sleeping household toward her room with the aid of a pen light.

Once there, I was supposed to help her pack her things in the large camper's backpack I'd bought for her. It had to be done by "an expert," Fausta had insisted. She had many things she wanted to bring, things that would have to serve her "all the way around the world backwards."

I was not to worry about the servants or Fausta's parents. They were "sound asleep every night by eleven o'clock."

Yet, when I reached Fausta's room, the door was not open a crack, as she had promised. I tried it, but found it locked, and there was no light inside.

Just as sad and bitter enlightenment dawned upon me, just as I was about to bolt down the stairs for the street, I was transfixed by a powerful flashlight beam, and someone shouted, *"Non muovere! Polizia! Polizia!"*

I looked for Fausta, as I reached for the sky, but she was nowhere to be found.

Cuffed in the rear of the *polizia municipale's* purple Alfa Romeo sedan, racing across a sleeping Naples toward the police station, I marveled at my own willful naïveté: Here I was, nearly twenty-seven years old. I had worked in a notorious prison and hitchhiked halfway 'round the world. Why, therefore, had I allowed myself to be duped by the silly and obvious ploy of a vengeful eighteen-year-old?

"*The truth of every passion wants some pretense to make it live,*" said Joseph Conrad.

But this went far beyond mere pretense. It was but one of the many clever traps I have set for myself, all through my life. The truth is that I have repeatedly contrived with my subconscious to expose and punish my own feverish behavior. Though I appear to have acquired a certain tolerance for my sins, I always manage to arrange for payment, one way or the other. And the interest will mount throughout my life.

I was sentenced to three months in Poggioreale City Prison for "breaking and entering," with credit for a month in jail awaiting trial.

In Naples at that time, inmates were not provided with meals by the city government. That responsibility fell upon the family of the incarcerated. If there was no family, inmates were permitted to order food from a local restaurant and pay to have it brought in. If neither of these options was available, the only sustenance provided was tepid water and day-old pasta from a local Catholic charity. Since I had been relieved of all my money and travelers' checks on my date of entry, and they never reappeared, I fell into the latter category.

Added to this, I was locked in solitary confinement, in the deepest, darkest, dankest dungeon of the ancient stone prison for the entire duration of my sentence. And my only contact with the outside world was a bald, muscular jailer with bulging gonads and an unreadable face—a dead-ringer for my old man, the prison guard.

The one thing they left me was my journal, and I wrote furiously in it all day, every day.

Under such conditions, and with nothing but time on my hands, one would imagine I might create something profound, some great dark work of prison fiction like Dostoevsky's *"Notes from the Underground."* Instead, everything I wrote in my journal at that time was utter self-pitying drivel.

To make things worse, I was plagued by the recurrent nightmare which has haunted me, off and on in various manifestations, all my life, especially when I find myself confined in some way:

My testicles are sliced off. I look down at them where they lie on the dirt floor of my Uncle Tom's tool shed, and they are like two broken eggs without their shells, whites and yokes intermingled. Two long, blood-red tendrils, like threads of living flesh, extend from the coalesced eggs to a single thick, bent, black, pubic hair as tall as a small tree. The tendrils hang in curlicues and are festive in appearance, like something one might drape over a Christmas tree. Meanwhile, somewhere in the background, an announcer keeps repeating a refrain in the homely Southwestern drawl of my father:

If the rock falls on the egg, alas.
If the egg falls on the rock, alas.

Every morning, it seemed, I was awakened from this dream by my jailor. Every morning, I mistook him at first for my father, and pleaded with him, "Why? Why? What have I done to deserve this kind of treatment?"

Only on the morning of my release did he reply.

"*La unica cosa che so è*... The only thing I know is I'm supposed to give you this on the day you leave," he said, and handed me a note.

The handwriting was Fausta's, and it can be translated thus:

Revenge is a fruit
Best left to ripen.

I could not see it then, but maybe Fausta was right, for her brother Marco was dead within the decade of a drug overdose. And when a mutual Italian friend ran into Fausta on Capri, thirty years after the fact, she was the image of her corpulent mamma...

You cannot make this stuff up: A year or so later, I found myself without funds again, living in a tiny, heatless, waterless, maid's room, a sixth-floor walk-up on the *rue Claude Bernard*. Just behind me, out my one little window, in the chill and rain of an April in Paris, lay the garden of the *College des Arts et Metiers*, full of blossoms, sprouting green grass and Galatean nymphs sculpted in the twenties as life-like replicas of silent movie queens.

I liked this garden and liked my window. When I required diversion from my squalid, little room, I could view the magnificent old *Beaux Arts* college across the garden, or the dome of the *Pantheon* over a half kilometer of tin Paris rooftops. The dome was located just across the square from the *Pantheon-Sorbonne,* where for three hundred old francs an hour, the equivalent of sixty cents, I taught English to graduate students eight hours a week, and from the *Foyer des Etudiants,* where for another 300 francs a night, one-eighth my weekly wage, I had dinner and wine.

One night, at about eight o'clock, I was looking out my window at the *College des Arts et Metiers* when I noticed that it was all lit up for a party. The sight got me excited, as if I were among the invitees: Now they were hanging red and blue lights!

I stood there watching the preparations for an hour until, at nine o'clock, the students began to arrive with their dates. All were dressed to kill: the girls very French with high-piled hair, painted eyes, stilettos held together with tiny straps; the boys with their pipes and puckered lips, their raincoats hanging over their shoulders, their *foulards* round their necks.

Watching, fascinated, I forgot the cold, the damp, the smell of the WC two doors down, the dirty washbasin on my desk, my wastebasket overflowing with rotting orange peels and old yoghurt cartons turning green. I ignored my soggy, concave bed, my piss-yellow wallpaper.

Forgetting all the things nagging at me, making me unhappy, uncomfortable, lonely, I entered that gay, lighted world across the garden, took a lovely French art student by the arm of my imagination, then wheeled her out on the floor for a waltz.

For a while, that was almost enough, but by ten o'clock I had become like one possessed. I had to get out of my cold, damp room with walls of piss, into that happy world across the garden.

Running into the WC, I filled my pot with icy water and shaved with a dull blade, cutting my neck in my haste.

Dressed in my best, a frayed white shirt, a ragged tartan tie, baggy grey tweeds, holey socks, shoes which had once been brown suede, I skipped down six flights of stairs, burst out the front door, and raced onto the *rue Claude Bernard*. Rounding the corner onto *rue Saint Jacques*, I stepped into a puddle, splashing my shoes with mud, but it didn't even slow me down.

Up the crowded front stairs of the *College des Arts et Metiers*. A bit out of breath, but suavely now, conscious of every step.

Spotting two unescorted girls just ahead, I slyly endeavored to be linked with them in the eyes of the two formidable door attendants.

Hesitation. Panic. Whip around. Proceed rapidly back down the stairs. Sneak a peek over the shoulder.

Damn! They weren't even interested in me!

But it was too late now. Blood on my collar. Mud on my shoes. No place to go. . . .

Just then, when I had reached my absolute nadir, I heard a female voice from behind me somewhere.

"Ernesto!"

I turned, and there she was before me, Danielle de Montigny, more beautiful than any Pygmalion statue, with her hair piled on her head, theatrical make-up, a long, mink coat, and glittering, high-heeled shoes.

"My god, Danielle! Where the hell did you come from?"

"J'étais juste entrain d'entrer avec des amis et . . . I was just going inside with some friends and I saw you."

"How did you even know me?"

"You, Ernesto? How could I forget you? You were famous in Positano."

"I was? For what?"

"For being like a bird dog," she said, giggling, "with all the girls on the beach!"

"Anyway," I put in, to change the subject, "so, you go to school here?"

"Yes, Tim and I . . ."

"Tim?"

"We have reconciled," she said, winking. "Didn't you know?"

"I had no idea. Where's Tim now?"

"In San Francisco. As soon as I finish the crash course in Interior Design that I am taking here, he will come to Paris. We shall go into business together."

"Well, stranger things have happened, I guess," I observed, shaking my head. "I heard what happened with you and—"

"Marco? He was never more than a fling. We Frenchwomen must have our flings, *n'est-ce pas?* Listen, how would you like to be my guest at the ball tonight?"

"Oh, Danielle . . ." I sighed. "You cannot know how much that would please me!"

"*Vous savez, monsieur,*" she whispered, taking my arm, flirting, inimitably French, bumping her hips against mine as we entered the brilliantly lit ballroom, "Tim mentioned that I should look you up. He thought you might squire me about, since I find myself alone in Paris."

"*Ma chère Danielle,*" I replied, ever the gallant, "nothing could please me more."

After we had dropped Danielle's coat off, after we'd had a couple of drinks and slipped into the restroom with one of her classmates for a snort of cocaine, I realized all my fantasies of earlier in the evening by whirling her out on the floor for a dance.

Then another couple of drinks. Another snort.

Another dance.

One thing led to another, and we ended up in my tiny room at four o'clock in the morning.

"Well, my husband wanted you to take care of me," said Danielle, laughing gaily, as I lay her down on my rank sagging bed. "But I'm not sure he had exactly this in mind."

"Don't be too sure of that," I said, sniffing in derision.

I took my time removing her clothes because she had the most spectacular body I had ever personally contemplated, and I wanted to do its beauty justice. First, the mink coat, then the sparkling dancing shoes, then the party dress. Danielle's skin was dark, and its contrast to her white panties and bra was breathtaking. I buried my nose in the fragrant cleft between her bounteous breasts. Ran it across to the ripe olives that showed through her bra. Gnawed at them through the fabric. When I decided that this turned her on, I slid my lips down her belly to the crotch of her panties and grated my teeth over the fabric till she started to pant and pull my hair. When I'd finally got her all spread apart, I commenced blowing and woofing at her through her now sopping panties, causing her to arch and strain into my face, smearing it with her excitement.

"Now fuck me!" she cried. *"Baise moi!"*

And I did exactly as she requested.

Indeed, I complied with all her wishes, all through the night.

Like many ladies of the Gallic persuasion, Danielle wanted it up the bum from time to time.

Another of her addictions was amphetamines.

When we picked up her husband up at Orly two months later, I had lost ten pounds, I had the shakes, I'd become a compulsive lotus eater, and I was delighted to hand her over, though there could be no question that hers was the most perfect body in all of existence.

I recall little else of my time with Danielle save for one thing.

After every bout of insane lovemaking, she would pout her pretty lips and whimper, in the voice of a lost little girl, *"Mais j'ai la cafard . . . but I've got the blues!"*

As I said before, you just can't make this stuff up. . . .

One cloudy afternoon in early June of that same year, I was walking across the Pont Royal, returning from an appointment with a married lady on the Right Bank (another story), when I heard a couple arguing on the Quai Voltaire below me, shouting at the tops of their lungs.

"Va te fair enculer!" she screamed at him.

"Fuck you too, bitch!" he hollered back.

Glancing down, I was shocked to discover that the ruckus was being caused by my two old friends Tim and Danielle, and that Tim was threatening to jump into the Seine.

"I swear, I'll do it! I'll do it!"

"Go on, you coward, do me a favor!"

Given their history as a couple, I was not altogether surprised at the scene. Since Tim's return from San Francisco, they had become notorious among our Left Bank set for their passionate dustups. Nor was this the first of Tim's suicide threats. At one recent party, I recalled, he became so infuriated when he caught Danielle dirty dancing with a mutual friend (yours truly, I'm afraid) that he ran out onto the fifth-floor terrace, threw a leg over the balustrade, and was on the point of jumping when stopped by a crowd of his friends.

This theatrical aspect of Tim's character was something I found alarming because I had never detected it in the past. On the contrary, in Italy he had internalized his suffering to an unnatural degree. His recent behavior thus indicated a dangerous escalation of his distress over Danielle's serial infidelities and was therefore something to be taken very seriously indeed.

Crossing the bridge, I slowed my pace to debate for a moment whether I should call down at them to distract them from their argument, for it now seemed about to erupt into an all-out physical confrontation.

"I'll take you with me, goddamn you, Danielle! Don't think I won't!"

"Just try it, you little *pedé*! See what you get!"

Nevertheless, I decided that it was "really none of my business; probably not as serious as it looked; better to just let them work it out for themselves." Which was a rationalization reflecting the fact that arbitration in spats between lovers is profitless at best, and—as every police officer and prison guard knows—perilous at worst. I consoled myself for my cowardice with the thought that Danielle was "one tough cookie," and well able to take care of herself.

Just as I was reaching the end of the bridge, I heard a piercing scream. I mean a scream of such fearful intensity that it cut through all the traffic noises of Paris like an air raid siren.

"Non! Non! Non!"

Leaning over the railing, I saw Tim perched on the stone riverbank, making as if to leap in headfirst. There were several reasons why this was no joke. First, Tim was the only Californian I knew who couldn't swim a lick. Second, the Seine was in full spring flow, bursting its banks with snow run-off, with swirling white rapids, swept up trees and trash, more like a mountain torrent than its normal placid self. Not to mention the fact that in recent months poor Tim had become so utterly whacked out over Danielle that he might go through with it.

"Tim!" I yelled, racing down the stairs two at a time. "Stop it, man, stop!"

Reaching the Quai, sprinting across the cobbles, I saw that he'd taken my arrival as a threat, and had now enfolded Danielle in his arms.

"Stop right where you are, you son-of-a-bitch!" he shrieked. "Or I swear I'll take her with me!"

"Easy now, Tim. Take it easy," I responded, slowing my approach, stretching out a consoling hand. "Come on, man, let's talk this over, okay?"

His response was to only hold her tighter, to edge closer to the embankment. When I saw him bend his knees and turn slightly in preparation to jump, I grabbed Danielle's down jacket and pulled with all my might. At the same time, she stamped on his foot with her sharp, high heel and jabbed him in the ribs with an elbow. Surprised, he released his grip enough for her to escape his clutches, and she fell into my arms.

Meanwhile, Tim had lost his balance. He was now teetering on the edge, waving his arms wildly in the air. Holding Danielle in my arms, I caught his eye, and what I saw there was not fear, horror, anger, or astonishment. What I saw was a kind of cheap disappointment, a dashed hope that he could not take her with him. His self-absorption was so total that I wasn't even sure that he registered who I was anymore.

Then he appeared to relax, to accept his fate. He dropped his arms, stopped resisting gravity, just let himself go, and fell backwards without a sound. It seemed like an age before I heard the splash. I let go of Danielle and ran to the edge. Already, Tim had floated off a hundred feet in the raging flood. The only part of him visible was his thinning blond hair swirling on the muddy surface. Then he went under.

"Lemme go, Ernesto!" Danielle cried, wild-eyed. "I can save him! I know I can!"

But she made no move to escape my arms. I realized that she had no intention of following him in. A Latin gesture, it was only meant for show, to placate her conscience.

The Seine was renowned for its numerous suicides. For that reason, it had a special police unit, headquartered on the Île *de la Cité,* equipped with drag nets and swift rubber boats which could be dispatched at a moment's notice. They arrived a few minutes after my emergency call, launched their boat, set off downstream, and found Tim a half hour later, caught up in flotsam under the *Pont de Solferino.* They brought him up to the Quai, lifted him out with a rope and tackle, and threw him down on the cobblestones. His face was drained of color. There were green tendrils of underwater plant life caught in his hair. Danielle broke away from me, ran to him, fell to her knees beside him, threw her arms around him, kissed his muddy eyes, his pale cheeks, called his name—"Timmy, Timmy, Timmy!"—making a big show of it, quite aware of her audience.

I understood her completely. I am part-Latin myself. It was good for her. Part of the healing process. When she finally let him go, they hoisted him onto a gurney, carried him to a waiting ambulance, loaded him in, and drove away. Danielle asked if she could accompany him, but they refused.

An examining magistrate, who had arrived in a police Citroën, took our depositions right there on the Quai. A pair of fishermen had witnessed the altercation from beginning to end, and they testified that Tim's death was suicide, so the interrogation was strictly pro forma.

Within an hour the magistrate, the detectives, the uniformed police officers and the witnesses had all disappeared. Danielle and I were alone on the Quai, which was now being swept by wind and rain.

"Let's go," I said, and escorted her up to the *Rue de Bac*, where I bundled her into a taxi.

On the way to her apartment, I kept telling her a lie to make her feel better. "He looked so peaceful in the end," I said, nodding, smiling, "so peaceful, didn't he?"

"Oui, oui," she breathed. "He did, didn't he? At last, he's at peace."

But the truth was the poor fucker looked terrible, and his face wore a grotesque mask of agony and despair.

The irony was that Danielle inherited all of Tim's money. A double irony was that she—the hottest lady in France—would never remarry. And a triple irony was that she died young, of breast cancer, after dedicating herself to charitable societies, especially those devoted to children.

Chapter Twelve

Every woman's weak and willin'
When she meets the proper villain.
CLARENCE DAY, 1928

It all began with a composition entitled *The Story of My Life,* written by one of my students at the *Pantheon-Sorbonne,* a beautiful young woman named Benedita Chang. I learned from her story that she was twenty-six years old, born and raised in the Portuguese colony of Macao. She spoke Portuguese, French, German, Cantonese, and Mandarin, along with the English she was perfecting in my department. Her mother had died when she was born, but her father was Macao's most celebrated internist. Benedita hoped to attend medical school as well.

When she was a young teenager, her father bought the apartment downstairs for her personal use. Yet, she did not enjoy her freedom, she wrote, because she was lonely and jealous of his girlfriends, many of whom were her own age. As an act of rebellion, she left home when she was eighteen to work as a waitress in Lisbon. Later, she lived in Munich with her older sister, who was married to a Bavarian gynecologist, and took a nursing course at a medical training college. She came to Paris with her fiancé, a Pakistani obstetrician with French residency rights whom she had met in Munich.

Though Benedita's command of English grammar was mediocre in the beginning, she fulfilled her writing assignments with a close at attention to detail, a lively style, and a talent for offbeat anecdotes.

Far more important to me than her academic performance, I must admit, was the fact that she was a nurse (I've always had a thing for nurses). Not to mention the vivid actuality of her physical presence in my classroom. Long and lithe, with lush black hair, cat eyes, a lovely, delicate oval face, and dark golden skin, she favored high heels, skirts, and sweaters, while everyone else wore typical late sixties hippy garb.

Every day she took a seat in the first row, directly in front of me, and started swinging her shapely legs, beaming an amused smile at me from under small, round, lightly tinted reading glasses. Her writing skills were more than satisfactory, but she never failed to stay after all the other students had departed, asking me endless questions about her grammar and writing technique, standing too close, touching my sleeve too often.

At the end of the semester, she rushed up to my desk after our last class to present me with an expensive bottle of Port as a farewell gift.

"We have much fun in your class, *Mestre!*" she very carefully pronounced, in her soft, sibilant, Chinese Portuguese accent. "I love so the way you teach!"

"Does this mean I can look forward to seeing you in the front row of my Advanced Writing class next semester?"

"It mean you can look for more than that," she purred, looking up at me from beneath long, fluttering eyelashes. "If you want."

At the school party the following night, Benedita came swaying up to where I stood in a line of sober pedagogues and prevailed upon me to dance the *Lambada*. Wrapping her arms around my neck, pressing her body to mine, she brazenly thrust a single, supple leg between my thighs. Then, wriggling her hips and buttocks to the beat of the pulsing rhythm, she swung me out onto the crowded dance floor. Long before the number was over, we had thoroughly scandalized my staid colleagues, and things had gotten so hot between us that our clothes were glued together with sweat.

The next semester, Benedita was on my attendance roster as promised. When I strode into the classroom on the first night, she leapt from her seat, ran up to my desk, and danced an impromptu little samba of pleasure in front of me, singing, *"Boa vinda, meu mestre!"* while my other students looked on, pop-eyed, mouths agape. After class, she waited until all the other students had departed, then followed me out into the hall. Slipping her arm into mine as we made for the elevator, leaning her fragrant head upon my shoulder, she gazed up at me with such frank, ardent desire that I knew it was only a matter of time.

The next night after class, Benedita led me past the elevator into the fire exit stairwell. Stopping me just inside the doorway, she cocked her hip, looked up at me wistfully, pouted her pretty lips like a small girl, and breathed one word, "*Please...*"

Expecting a janitor to come upon us at any moment, yet unable to oppose her intentions a moment longer, I took her into my arms and kissed her tender little ears, the dark, furry, nape of her neck, the upward-slanting corners of her brown and yellow eyes. I inhaled the secret scent of her body and hair, the intoxicating chemical compounds that made her who she was, which instantly stimulated my own. And I felt their immediate effect with her racing pulse, her panting breath, her weakening knees. She offered her mouth. I licked her saffron lips, the honeyed tip of her tongue. Pursing her mouth, she slipped it between my teeth and wrapped it around my tongue like a hungry kitten.

We made such an incredible racket in the stairwell that night, moaning, groaning, banging against the wall, that I was sure that University Security would soon be upon us. Yet, for some reason, Lord Buddha chose to smile upon us.

On the way down in the elevator, Benedita smiled up at me naughtily, rolling her eyes.

"Why you resist me so long, Teacher? I do everything but strip naked last semester, but you like cold as stone."

"I felt it was unethical, for one thing," I replied, a bald-faced lie. "Not to mention your fiancé."

"Eh, certain things in life," she said, shrugging her delicate shoulders in a gesture more Latin than Asian. "*Que será, será,* you know?"

Waiting for us when we emerged from the elevator was Benedita's fiancé, a dark, bearded man in his mid-thirties, wearing pastel green medical scrubs.

"Mohammed!" she exclaimed delightedly, as if the mere sight of him were enough to send her into raptures.

Kissing him on either cheek, folding her small, yellow hand into his big brown one, she turned toward me, grinning as if it were the most natural thing in the world:

"*Caro*, I would like you to meet my professor."

"A pleasure," I said, attempting a smile.

"Ah, but the pleasure it is all mine, sir, I am sure," he replied, smiling ingratiatingly, while reaching out to shake my hand. "Mohammed Baluchi, MD, at your service!"

The next night, after class, I said to her, "I bet you fucked his brains out as soon as you got home, right?"

"*Naturalmente*," she retorted, laughing unapologetically. "You get me so ... *whoo!*"

"Women's powers of duplicity always amaze me."

"Hey, you got the wrong idea, Teacher," she said. "What I got with him, what I got with you, they are two different things, but they are both real."

For months, we carried on our affair, yet there was always a certain distance between us. Benedita never called me anything but "Teacher," "Professor," or the intoxicating *"Meu Mestre."* I never called her anything other than Senhorita Chang; though I admit we uttered our formal titles with a certain irony, and they merely added to our illicit pleasure in each other.

Frankly, this was no love match. We didn't really talk, and I never learned much more about her than I did from reading her first essay. I had no idea of her life outside of class. And I knew nothing of her relationship with her fiancé. Nor did she know more about me than what I revealed to my students at large. I told her nothing of my private life, my friends and fellows, my intellectual pursuits. The truth was our passion for each other was purely carnal, the result of a chemical reaction utterly beyond our control. But once that dopamine started popping, damn! It was exceedingly difficult to contain, or even to explain.

Benedita was committed, even devoted, to her partner, but she felt zero guilt. We could not have been more different. Yet, the fact that we led totally separate lives, knew little about each other, shared no interests other than sex, simply added to the dramatic effect. Benedita had clearly fulfilled some very deep-seated psychological compulsion by seducing her teacher, and he had done the same by succumbing.

That our actions were unethical was just frosting on the cake. On some level, we both craved retribution for sins of the subconscious which had little or nothing to do with our present misconduct.

God knows how long the affair might have continued, were it not for the intervention of fate. One morning, I picked up the International Herald Tribune and glanced at a headline on the fourth page of the Metro section:

YOUNG IMMIGRANT DIES
IN CUT-RATE ABORTION CLINIC.

"Dr. Mohammed Baluchi, of 67 Boulevard Vincent Auriol, 13th Arrodissement, Paris, has been named in the investigation, along with his nurse, Ms. Benedita Chang, of the same address," I read; and by now, my attention had become fully engaged. Adding to my shock and dismay was the District Attorney's assertion, quoted later in the article, that "this is not the first suspicious death at the clinic, and there is some question as to the authenticity of the credentials of both the doctor and his nurse."

After the newspaper report, Benedita ceased coming to class, and I read nothing more about the case.

I gave it a week, then sent her a note on *Sorbonne Pantheon* stationary. Three days later, she replied with a dry little note stating that she and Mohammed were caught up in a criminal proceeding and had to spend all their time defending themselves. She had no more time for "hanky-panky," as she put it.

"And so, Ernesto, I guess this must serve as our farewell. *Adeus, meu mestre, e boa fortuna!*"

I took it much harder than I thought I would. Far from being shocked by Benedita's alleged criminal activities, I was even more intrigued by her now. And I never ceased wondering how anyone so lovely, with whom I had spent so many enchanting moments, could be mixed up in anything so vile. In short, I missed the girl more than I ever thought I might. And I took to drinking far more than I should have to expunge her hauntingly beautiful physical presence from my mind.

Twenty-five years later, I was on a train in Germany, heading to Budapest, Hungary, where my daughter, the actor Lucia Brawley, was starring in a film called LORA.

And guess who swung into the seat right next to me?

Benedita Chang, looking just as beautiful as ever.

"Professor?" she exclaimed, looking over at me through those same little round tinted reading glasses. "Is that you? Wow, you lose all your hair!"

"Time tells," I said, shrugging it off. "How are you, Senhorita Chang?"

"You want to know the truth?" she replied. "Not so good."

"What happened with your fiancé," I inquired. "And that trouble with the clinic?"

"We won the case. Settled out of court. But then he went back to Pakistan," she said, pausing significantly, then turned to gaze up at me in genuine, almost tearful distress. "To marry a girl his family arranged. Thing is, though, he didn't tell me about it till the day he left—big surprise."

"I'll bet. What've you been doing since then?"

"Me?" she said, trying a smile. "Oh, this and that. Worked in Portugal a few years. Now Germany. Staying with my sister. Looking for a job."

"As a nurse?"

"Maybe not."

"Would you like to have lunch with me in the dining car, and share a bottle of wine?" I asked, looking her over, smelling her, the dopamine starting to pop again, after all those years, yet feeling genuine compassion for her. "Maybe I can cheer you up."

"*Obrigada*, but no," she sighed, rising to leave her seat. "You always taught us English expressions in class, right?"

"Right."

"Remember the one, 'water under the bridge?'"

Chapter Thirteen

Mystery magnifies danger as the fog the sun.
Charles Caleb Colton, 1825

A few months after I left Paris, I was hitching across the Middle East with a big, tough, Austro-Slovenian lesbian named (believe it or not) Eva Braun. We had tied up together in Bucharest, Romania, shortly after I was released from prison there (another story), and I found her to be an excellent hitchhiking mate, though neither of us spoke more than a few words of the other's language, and our relationship was strictly platonic. She was certainly better than any man I'd ever hitched with. She kept her mouth shut, shared what she had, never whined, or complained, and was very good in a fight.

One time I recall, we were stuck out in the middle of the Great Salt Desert of Iran, between Tehran and the Afghan border. We had spent eight hours at this same desolate crossroad, with the wind blowing potassium iodide in our faces. It was late at night, getting colder by the minute, and the jackals were howling.

Suddenly, from across the western desert, we heard an engine approaching, heading east, our desired direction. Then, lights out, a big, long bus pulled up beside us in a swirl of brackish white dust.

The door swung open. We climbed aboard. The bus took off again. And we found ourselves among a group of men who seemed as if they had just stepped out of the pages of the Quran. In their keffiyehs, curly black beards, and long robes, they looked like they ought to be riding camels, not a modern bus.

Sidling rearward to find a seat, I tried to puzzle things out. What I found truly odd was that our fellow passengers completely ignored us, though we stuck out among them—especially Eva—like a pair of sore thumbs. The reason they ignored us, we quickly determined, was that they were mumbling Islamic prayers and fingering prayer beads, led by an old, white-bearded holy man called a "Mullah" who was sitting across the aisle from us.

After a few minutes, the young fellow sitting behind us tapped me on the back. "You mind, sir, I practice my English with you?" he asked, and we were rapidly enlightened. "We are pilgrims," he said, "going for the holy city of Meshed, on the Afghani border."

"Ach, zo!" Eva exclaimed.

And we quickly relaxed. He fed us tea, grapes, and nuts. We settled in, told ourselves how lucky we were to be getting a free ride all the way across the Great Salt Desert.

Exhausting our English-speaking friend's vocabulary within a matter of minutes, and with nothing else to while away the hours, we set our minds to the problem of understanding our driver and his relationship to the highway. It was very narrow, with only one lane and deep drainage ditches on either side, yet no one used headlights. We found this so puzzling that we asked our English-speaking friend.

"Well, of course," he replied, as if we were impossibly obtuse, "they do it to save electricity."

Whatever the truth of the matter, when two vehicles approached each other, they detected one another not by sight, but by sound or shadow. Then they blinked their lights furiously at each other and—according to some rule of the desert that I didn't quite understand at first—one of them deferred to the other, pulled over to the side at one of the strategically placed wide shoulders, and let the other pass.

Since ours was by far the largest vehicle on the road, and all the others we met deferred to our driver's blinking lights, I inferred after a time that the rule was this: "Might Maketh Right." So, our driver put his gas pedal to the floor and never touched his brake all night, for any reason. Any dog or sheep in the road was dead meat. If there was a shepherd in the way, he'd better keep his ear to the ground and jump fast.

Things went along like this for a few hours. We started to doze off, but a commotion woke us a bit before dawn when our fellow passengers started whispering and gesturing to each other anxiously. We looked ahead to determine what the trouble might be and saw an even *bigger* bus coming at us out of the darkness, about three kilometers away. Both drivers were blinking their lights furiously at each other, but our driver—apparently some kind of macho man—refused to defer as he ought. Meanwhile, we were approaching each other at a combined speed of a hundred miles an hour.

Just when Eva and I were about to give into despair, the old Mullah suddenly rose from his seat beside us and waddled up the aisle to the driver. We felt relieved, for we assumed that the religious leader would now instruct the driver to pull over, stop, and let the other bus pass, as he should.

Yet, the Mullah did nothing of the sort. Ignoring the driver, he wheeled toward the rear of the bus, stretched his arms to the roof, and screamed at the top of his lungs, *"Allah!"*

To which everyone else on the bus, including the driver, Eva, and me, shouted in reply, *"Salaam!"*

"Allah!"

"Salaam!"

"Allah, Salaam!"

We all kept screaming, praying that Allah would deliver us from death, since the driver and the Mullah certainly would not.

Unfortunately, however, Allah did not seem to be listening to our prayers, for now the other bus seemed about to slam into us headfirst.

Eva and I dropped our heads to our knees, squeezed our eyes shut, and prepared to die instantly.

Then we heard something that sounded like "Whoosh!"

We pinched our skin. We were still alive! We looked out the back and saw, against all the laws of physics, the bigger bus rapidly departing westward down the narrow road to Tehran.

"*Gross Got!*" Eva exclaimed.

"What happened?" I asked our English-speaking friend.

"I don't know!" he said, laughing, delighted at his own continued existence. "But I'm happy it did—whatever it was!"

"Ask the Mullah," I said.

So, he turned to the holy man—who had returned to his seat across the aisle and now emanated serene unconcern—and said a few words in Farsi. In reply, the Mullah pointed up at the sky and said something very serious.

"What's he say?" I asked.

"He says it was 'the hand of Allah.'"

"The . . . what?"

"The hand of Allah," the young man repeated.

"I don't understand."

"Neither do I."

"Well, ask him, please."

He did as I said, and this was the Mullah's reply, as translated to Eva and me:

"*The two buses were coming together. We were all going to die, but we prayed to Allah and He heard. He reached His hand down from heaven and picked up our bus, holding us suspended above the highway until the other bus had passed beneath us. Then He placed us back down on the road as gently as a lamb, and we sped on our way.*"

And did we believe him? You bet we did!

It was truly the hand of Allah.

Chapter Fourteen

*The rose's scent is bitterness
to him that loved the rose.*
Francis Thompson, 1890

After Eva and I had crossed into pre-Taliban Afghanistan—where the girls in Kabul wore miniskirts instead of hijabs—we crossed the yellow plains of Pakistan with two lecherous, omni-sexual truck drivers, the last in a long line of them that stretched back across all the lands of Islam.

At the Indian border, though, near Amritsar, the authorities refused to let me in without a visa. When I enquired where I might obtain one, they informed me that the only consulate in Pakistan capable of issuing me an Indian visa was in Karachi, a thousand-mile hitchhike to the south. From there, I learned I could book a passage to Mumbai by sea.

I was not particularly disappointed by this news because I had already come nine thousand miles from Paris, most of it over rough roads, so what was another thousand miles?

Besides, I had long since learned that I could count on every detour in my travels to provide me with new adventures.

I bade *adieu* to Eva, who unexpectedly cried in my arms and pressed her Ljubljana address upon me.

Then I turned to cross the no-man's-land between the Indian and Pakistani borders. Escorted by two young Pakistani soldiers, I made my way for several yards along a tall fence lining the frontier.

And there I was afflicted with the second great fever of my life. She was hanging on the fence, smiling at me.

"*D'ou venez-vous, monsieur?*"

"*Californie,*" I replied, stopping in my tracks, winking at my grinning, indulgent military escorts. "*Et vous, mademoiselle?*"

"I'm from Belgium," she replied, with only the slightest, most seductive accent in English. "I saw you at the border post and followed you here. I was impressed by your *detachment*, your *insouciance*. Anyone else would have been bitterly disappointed and caused a big row, but you simply kissed your girlfriend goodbye and . . ."

"She's just a friend, a hitchhiking mate."

"Well, anyway, you seemed so philosophical about it all."

By then, I had approached the fence, with the blessing of my guards, and was hanging on the wire with my hands very close to hers.

"I was intrigued by your beard, your backpack . . . your well-traveled air," she said, echoing another pretty girl, Fausta, at the other end of the Great Grass Road. "Have you been at it long?"

"Yes, quite long," I replied. "Over two years, now."

"You're going all the way round the world?"

"Yes, backwards."

"You mean . . . ?"

"I can't exactly put it into words," I explained. "It's probably more metaphorical than factual. Maybe, it's just a way of reminding myself that I'm . . . that I'm doing it in my own unique way, not the way other people do. Or maybe it's a kind of Confucian logic. You know—circular logic? Maybe I'm going around the world to find out where I'm coming from. You know what I mean?"

"Yes, I think I do," she said. "And you know, in that case, I think I might be going around the world backwards, too. Except, I've got a bit of money from *mon père, tu vois?* So, I don't have to auto-stop. Mostly I take trains and buses. Sometimes even planes. I must say, the idea of hitchhiking around South Asia is rather frightening to me. But it might be fun in a safe place like Japan, don't you think?"

By then, my military escorts were starting to get restless.

Realizing that time was of the essence, we glommed onto every word, peering deeply into the other's eyes, trying to size each other up in the few moments that we had left.

There could be no question but that it was instant, reciprocal, made especially compelling by the time element, the fence separating us, and the fact that we might never see each other again.

Now my escort was tugging at my sleeve, and we were suddenly almost desperate. We groped for each other's hands through the fence and came within an inch of kissing.

"Where are you headed next?" she asked.

"Karachi," I replied.

"I'll drop you a line in care of American Express," she promised, breathlessly, as they started to lead me away. "Let's hitchhike around Japan together; what do you say?"

"Let's do it!"

"What's your name?" she shouted after us.

"Ernesto Brawley! What's yours?"

"Eugènie Voet!" she screamed, jumping up and down behind the fence. "How do you spell your last name?"

I spelled it out for her as loudly as I could, but I was not sure she got it, for by then we were quite a distance off.

Of course, this only made it all more feverish.

So, all the way down to Karachi along the scorched plains of the Indus River Valley I went over our meeting in my mind.

The little frock that Eugènie had worn was so clean, so fresh—an off-white traveling dress, light cotton for the tropics—and it fit so nicely round her firm high breasts, tiny waist, swelling hips, long shapely legs. Her ash-blond hair hung just above the shoulder, so shiny and shampooed that it flounced every time she nodded her head.

How long had it been since I had seen anyone like Eugènie? With her translucent, blue-veined skin, round cerulean eyes, long lids, tipped-up nose, rosy cheeks, pale lips, and pointed chin, she looked like a time traveler, a girl who had just stepped out of a Flemish painting.

"Are you some kind of artist?" I had asked at one point; but I was merely flattering her, for what she really looked like was an artist's model from the Renaissance.

"I'm a classical pianist," she replied, speaking quickly, urgently, yet enunciating every word precisely. "Just finished six years of *hautes études* at the *Consérvatoire de Bruxelles*. This trip around the world is my graduation gift."

Yet, there was something very sensible about her as well: That traveling frock, those neat white sneakers. Her handshake, so firm and dry. And her name, Eugènie, so impossibly outdated, so *Empire*, that it had a kind of old-fashioned charm.

In Karachi, I expected nothing; I was therefore especially delighted to find a note from her awaiting me at American Express. Like all the notes I have received, from all the girls I have known, I stuck it in the appropriate page of my journal, and I have kept it there for sixty years.

> *Cher monsieur:*
> *C'est moi, Eugènie. ¿Te rappelles tu? C'était à la frontière. ¡Vive l'American Express!* Ernesto, it occurs to me that you know absolutely nothing about me, nothing of my likes, dislikes, personal tastes. I love late Renaissance music, Orlandus, Lassus, Palestrine, Baroque in Germany. In this century: Stravinsky, Prokofieff, Bartok, Hindemith. I also love traveling, and I absorb everything, enough to last a lifetime. I adored Old Delhi, the Taj Mahal... and so many other things.... Why can I not just come out and say what is on my mind? I can't stop thinking about you! Do you

feel the same? Yet how can it be? We only met
for a moment. . . .

I fired off an answer to Eugènie expressing like sentiments, requesting a meeting in Mumbai, at American Express, at a specific hour in two weeks' time.

In the Port of Karachi, I ran into another backpacker named Misty Thorssen. A spectacular redhead with opaque eyes and sleep-walker's gait of a heavy drug user, she said she was on her way to Goa to meet some business friends. Though I had no doubt what her business was, it did nothing to put me off. Indeed, in that era, in that part of the world, at that period of my life, I would have been surprised if she did anything else.

After quickly conferring, we decided to book deck passage together on the Indian ship, *Sabarmati*, bound for the Rann of Kutch, Mumbai, and Goa. To save money, and to see a bit of the country, I would disembark in the Rann of Kutch then make my way overland to Mumbai. Misty would stay aboard for the leg to Mumbai and Goa.

Perhaps the most remarkable part of our three-day voyage across the Arabian Sea—aside from the eerie effects of Misty's stash of Afghan hash, and our nightly lovemaking on the heaving deck—was at the very end, when three long, graceful, swallow-sailed boats came flying out to meet us in the Rann of Kutch to pick up passengers for the shallow-draft port at Kutch Mandvi. They made a beeline for us, as if they might crash directly into the bulkhead. Then, at the very last instant, in perfect coordination, they jerked their rudders full right, dropped sails, and bounced gently up beside us, buffered by the back wash of their own wakes.

Blowing a kiss to Misty, I tossed my rucksack into one of the boats, jumped down after it into a veritable sea of black flesh, then we skimmed off across the muddy waters of the estuary. I disembarked on the beach at Kutch Mandvi, a town of such malodorous filth and poverty that I left it instantly.

Walking, hitchhiking, riding rupee buses, I spent the next three days making for the railhead at Ahmedabad. This was the India I had thrilled to, when I imagined it in California: naked, devout Hindus performing their ablutions in rivers of steaming excreta. Lean black *Sadus* and rickshaw *wallahs* squatting in the dirt. Bony, white Brahma cows wandering the byways. Beggar boys with limbs intentionally torn and twisted at birth, scuttling along the gutters like wounded insects. Dead animals in the streets. The sickly-sweet smell of decaying flesh. Fat black flies. Lush maggots. Long white worms. Great carrion birds circling overhead, swooping to partake of the feast: "*Dead breaths I living breath*" the master said, "*tread dead dust, devour a ruinous offal from all dead.*" And everywhere people, masses of dark sweating Indians, crowding, bumping, jostling, butt to butt, belly to belly. Eating, sleeping, rutting, fucking, spitting, puking, pissing, and shitting, they swarmed over every square inch of real estate. The only muck I found lacking was table garbage; it being gobbled up before it hit the ground.

By the time I reached the railroad station, I had seen enough to last a lifetime.

Other hitchhikers had told me that one need never pay for a ticket on Indian Railways. You just rush the train along with the swarming natives, climb aboard, then hang on for dear life. But I refined the technique. I dressed in my best (having long since found it expedient to keep a clean white shirt and bush jacket rolled up in my backpack) then found a place in first class. When the conductor came round, I said, in my rough approximation of a posh Brit accent, "Frightfully sorry, old chap, but I seem to have misplaced my ticket." The older conductors had been around since the days of the Raj; it was apparently second nature for them to jump to attention when they heard that kind of crisply spoken English. Whatever the case, it never seemed to occur to them that a pukka Sahib such as I might possibly consider breaching his code of honor. In short, I rode into Mumbai in style.

I checked into a cut-rate Salvation Army hostel in the port district, near Fort Point and the Gateway to India. My room was dorm-style, a bargain at ten rupees a night (fifty cents American), and I bedded amid lean, young, hippy hitchhikers like me from every corner of the globe.

As always, we rapidly exchanged notes on our travels to obtain useful information from fellow wanderers moving in the opposite direction. We offered few tips on scenic areas, museums, art galleries, or cultural activities, for we were not so interested in sightseeing *per se* as in putting a lot of cross-country kilometers under our belts, experiencing Third World life up close and personal, while marveling at our own daring-do. Confronted by a huge, bustling, modern city like Mumbai, we tended to float, to indulge ourselves in a bit of well-earned R & R.

The world is very large when you look at it on an atlas, but our world was so small that we kept bumping into each other all the time.

Two of the backpackers I ran into at the hostel, a pair of muscular Israelis, I had last seen in Santa Cruz, Bolivia. Several others I crossed paths with on the Great Grass Road from Europe. There was even one bloke, a London Cockney, who knew Carol and me when we were bartending at the Casa Campello; and he wanted to know, "Where's she got to then, mate?"

"Sorry, 'aven't the foggiest," I replied, mocking his accent, a bit defensively, I admit.

Two mornings later, I hurried to American Express, at Church Gate.

And Eugènie was waiting for me, just inside the door.

In a blue polo shirt, a tan polished-cotton skirt, and white tennis shoes, she was such a perfect picture of preppy Euro perkiness that I instantly committed it to memory.

She was so excited to see me that she nearly danced across the marble floor to greet me; and the perfunctory buss on either cheek that was *de rigeur* became a lingering kiss that set the middle-aged patrons gaping.

She smelled so good that I could have eaten her on the spot.

We strolled hand-in-hand to an English tea shop near St. George's Church, chatting, laughing about absolutely nothing. We seated ourselves at a corner wicker table, ordered a pot of Earl Grey with milk, honey and scones, then put our heads together.

"I have imagined so many things," Eugènie sighed, fixing those azure-hued eyeballs upon me, entwining her cool long fingers in mine.

"I've built it up in my mind to such an extent that it's like this whole great edifice that I'm afraid is top-heavy. Soon it might just collapse, come tumbling down on top of me."

"I know exactly what you mean," I said.

"It happened the first instant I saw you," she went on. "I don't know how, but I knew immediately that you were the one. It was like *un coup de foudre*. You know? Just hit me. But afterwards, on the way to Delhi, I could not trust my instincts. So, I started to doubt, to tell myself what a silly girl I was."

"I had no doubts at all," I put in, lying through my teeth. "But I hear what you're saying."

"So now?" she asked. "What?"

"So now we just see what happens, right?"

"Okay, but I tell you what, Ernesto. I think I need time to sort it all out in my mind. You know what I mean? Now that I've seen you, *je perdre la tête, tu sais?* I am freaking out. Feel my heart. You see? It's beating so hard I'm afraid I'm going to have some kind of heart attack. Maybe we should just call it a day."

"What?" I demanded. "What?"

"Go home to our hotels and reflect," she replied, staring into my eyes. "Put our thoughts in order. Write each other a letter explaining how we feel. Meet tomorrow and exchange them. *Qu'est-ce que t'en penses?*"

"If you insist," I said, after absorbing the meaning of her words.

Then I took a deep breath and continued, "I ask only one thing, Eugènie, before you go. In the lobby of the Salvation Army Hostel, they've got an old baby grand, the bequeathal of an Anglo-Indian lady. It's not perfectly in tune, but I'd like you to play it for me. Just one piece. Whatever you like. Would you do that for me?"

"*Avec plaisir, mon coucou,*" she said, grinning with delight.

So, we went back to Fort Point. Eugènie played Robert Schumann's "*Davidsbündlertänze*" on the rickety old piano, and I had never heard anything so lovely in my life.

I saw her back to her little hotel near the Prince of Wales Museum, and retired to my thoughts, the principal among which was: *What am I going to do with this girl? I haven't got any money!*

I had a talk with my cohorts at the hostel and discovered that there was in fact a way to earn money in Mumbai. Apparently, there was a Goan-Indian named João de Mèndes, a man of unsavory reputation, who lived out near Breach Kandy and recruited young foreigners as moneychangers for the tourist trade.

Late that afternoon, after the heat had subsided a bit, I rode the bus around Malabar Hill to Breach Kandy, near Mahalaxmi Temple, where I presented myself to João at his office across Marine Drive from the European Racket & Bathing Club.

João—or "Himself," as he was known in the neighborhood—turned out to be paunchy, fat, and very black. He sported an upswept walrus mustache and was quite well-spoken in Indian English.

After brief introductions, he accepted my application for employment, then gave me a quick background talk:

"Here in India, you see, one can only exchange foreign monies for rupees at official government sites. The catch being that they are offering a mere half the going rate. This is our opportunity, as the rupee is worthless on the international money market, and rich Indians are desperate for dollars and European currencies. Foreigners are likewise wanting, for they are not obtaining full value for their legal tender. Yet moneychangers of the Indian race, rightly or wrongly, are being handicapped by highly untrustworthy reputations. This, my dear pale-faced fellow, is where you are coming in. You will be getting a five percent cut on all the foreign monies you are exchanging, plus room and board, courtesy of yours truly. What are you thinking of this?"

"I'll take it!" I declared. "When do I start?"

"Why not right now?" he laughed. "We are conveniently locating just across the street from the biggest sports club in Mumbai. It is open exclusively to Caucasians (apparently, they are not wanting their 'waters muddied,' if you will excuse the jest), for which reason it is always full of fastidious tourists, plane crews, charity workers, visiting professors, UN people, along with some permanent foreign residents. And they are all, as you say, ripe for the fleecing.' You must simply be waiting outside, catching them as they are coming and going. Any questions?"

"No, sir," I replied. "I'll get right at it!"

And I earned five hundred rupees, quite a considerable sum in India, that very day.

The next morning, when I went to meet Eugènie at her hotel, there was a note awaiting me at the reception desk.

> *J'ai quitté Mumbai. Comprends-moi. Je suis trop embrouillé pour commencer...* I have left Mumbai. Understand me. I am too embroiled to commence. You see, it's not that easy—a dream constructed over years. *Est-ce la joie où la terreur? Vas-tu me creèr où me détruire en m'imprégnant de ta virilité?* Give me some time, Ernesto. I'll meet you in Calcutta on *25 Janvier*. I'll leave a note at American Express.
> *C'est moi, Eugènie.*

Oddly, I found Eugènie's letter to be a relief, for I had felt something of the same. More importantly, I had awakened that very morning with a raging dose of crab lice—not my first and unfortunately not my last—which I had picked up alone in my bed at the Salvation Army Hostel. I could hardly make love to Eugènie in this state, could I? Not to mention my embarrassing lack of funds.

Nevertheless, I had far too much experience of lovers' games to let her off the hook that easily, so I wrote her back c/o American Express in Madras, where I knew she was headed next:

> *You have killed me, Eugènie. It was so dishonest. How could you do it? I will be in Calcutta, but can I trust you to be there as well?*

I worked for Himself almost a month. It turned out that he was not only a moneychanger but also a bootlegger, dope dealer, gunrunner, loan shark and pimp. At the same time, he was a devout Catholic, an usher at the local Goan R.C. church who attended services daily. He was, moreover, the owner of a large compound near Cuffe Parade that consisted of a home for him and his huge extended family, a distillery, a restaurant, a brothel, and a warehouse for his contraband. Yet, he preferred to sleep not in his home but outside on the sidewalk because, as he said, "It's the only place for beating this confounding heat."

He shared this preference, or necessity, with thousands of other Indians in Mumbai, who clogged the sidewalks and even the side streets with their prone bodies at night. Thus, the "room" that I was offered "gratis" turned out to be a space on the sidewalk beside Himself, his pushers, bootleggers, foreign moneychangers, four of his whores, two German Shepherd dogs, and whatever itinerant beggar or *Sadu* turned up. At night, we passed around "The Gun," a powerful opium water pipe, while sipping at bottles of "Country," the potent local moonshine. Meanwhile, Himself's wife and daughters slept within the precincts of his vast firetrap of a wooden house, under finely woven mosquito nets that swayed like ghosts in gusts from the ceiling fan.

Out on the sidewalk, the air was like a hot, wet blanket. Breathing was like inhaling sulfur directly from the source. Liters of sweat poured off our par-boiled bodies. Vast coordinated formations of mosquitoes circled and dove in waves to buzzbomb every square centimeter of exposed flesh. Our feet hung over the narrow sidewalk, dipping into the ripe sweetness of the Mumbai gutter. Great gray rats, the size of cats, played footsy with our extremities. Sick babies wailed into the darkness. Husbands beat wives. Himself's harlots aired their quiffs beside us. While the high-pitched, otherworldly voices of female singers ululated their Hindi sorrows from dozens of portable radios at once. At dawn, when Mumbai awakened, its work-bound citizens came stepping over us in such hordes that they intruded upon our slumbering bodies, providing us with unwanted glimpses up their once-white dhotis and robes.

Yet, incredible as it may seem, waking on the sidewalk each morning I found myself immeasurably excited by the romantic adventure of where I was, and what—impossibly—I was doing.

Meanwhile I kept my nose clean, my mouth shut and saved every rupee I earned. I lost the crabs by shaving my pubes to the nub then dousing myself nightly with Himself's moonshine liquor, which, being almost pure rubbing alcohol, burnt like fire.

By the time I took my leave, on a First-Class Indian Railways sleeping car by way of Agra, Delhi, and Benares, with a brief smuggling run to Kathmandu at the behest of Himself (a story best left untold), my pockets were jingling with rupees and I was in fine fettle.

I arrived in Calcutta on the appointed date, then checked into the Sikh Temple, near Bara Bazaar. Like all Sikh Temples everywhere, it had a generous open-door policy for foreign backpackers.

After a quick, cold shower in the courtyard stall, I changed into my pukka best, checked my backpack in the beadle's office, then hastened toward American Express on Strand Road for my third meeting with Eugènie.

"Do I love you, or just the idea of you?" I kept asking myself on the way, my heart and mind racing in unison. "Am I deceiving myself out of loneliness? Once I obtain your love, Eugènie, will I value it less?"

Just as I was walking into American Express, her rickshaw pulled up in front.

"Ernesto!" she shrieked, and I dashed back down the stairs three at a time to sweep her into my arms.

"Oh, but you leave me weak," she gasped, and her knees gave way.

She went down on her knees before me again that night in our hotel, before we ever made love.

"Be good to me, Ernesto!" she cried, clasping her arms about my naked loins, pressing her face to my sex.

I raised her up to kiss her tears away but wondered for the first time whether I could trust Eugènie's sincerity, for some of her gestures seemed affected, even melodramatic. Then it struck me that there was something especially important about her that I did not yet know, something with which I might not be altogether pleased.

I wanted that first night to be perfect, to fit all the romantic scenarios which had sustained me across India. I wanted soft colors, a melting into the rhythm of love. But Eugènie wanted to talk nasty. She wanted me to tie her up and spank her. Lost in her own feverish pleasure, she did not look at me when we had sex. Her eyes rolled back in her head, and it was like she was doing it with herself. Then, when she really got hot, it was not like she was making love at all but having some kind of epileptic fit. Her pelvis came pounding up at me with unbelievable rapidity and ferocity, like a jackhammer, an uncontrollable reaction rather than an act of love. Although this might be exciting to a casual lover, it frightened and disillusioned a poetic soul like Ernesto, who had centered all his dreams on the enchanting Eugénie.

Yet, it was only our nights that I hated, for all our days were golden. We awakened happily in the mornings and tramped about seeing the sights, kissing, and giggling like a pair of honeymooners.

I recall with special pleasure a time, commemorated in a photo that I still have, when I was standing above Eugénie on a grassy knoll, with the mysterious temple of Kalighat Mandir behind us. Two great walled terraces fell away before us, grey with tropical years, their images reflected in a vast, lily-covered moat. With her camera in hand, Eugénie was looking up at me, smiling as sweetly and innocently as a little girl. About to snap my picture, she exclaimed, as if it had just occurred to her, "*Mais comme tu es beau!* But how handsome you are, Ernesto!"

The next day we rode six kilometers from our hotel by pedicab, the leisurely pace suiting us perfectly. We sniffed the air, the smell of jasmine and fresh new leaves, then turned to sniff each other.

"*Je suis si contente.*"

"*Moi aussi,*"

"*Dit moi, Ernesto,* what shall we name our children?"

"*Mais certainement!*" I said. "Tristán and Cybèle."

"*Mon dieu*, how did you know?" she marveled. "I picked those names when I was twelve years old!"

Later, we found a hidden arbor, to the rear of the bulbous temple of Dakshineswar Kali, where we lay together on the ancient pitted volcanic floor, staring up at the writhing, slithering, entwined black banyan roots that held up the stone ceiling.

"My God, Ernesto, how do they do it?"

"Haven't a clue," I said. "I'm a lover and a poet, not an engineer."

"Right, you're a poet and your feet show it," she replied with a laugh. "They're Longfellows!"

"Oh, Jesus, where do you get these stupid American jokes?" I scoffed. "That went out with my grandfather."

"Didn't I tell you? I did my senior year in high school with an exchange program in the United States."

"No, you didn't! Where did you go?"

"Altoona, Pennsylvania," she replied with a laugh.

"Holy shit! No wonder you're so fucked up!" I teased, then grabbed her, wrestled her over on top of me.

"I'll show you how fucking fucked up I am," she whispered, then unzipped my pants, pulled me out, gripping me tightly in her hand.

"Mmmm, now he's a Longfellow, too!" she exclaimed, and slipped me into her mouth.

We made love on the temple floor, and I told Eugénie I wanted it to go on forever. She responded with all her heart, and I saw pure, uncomplicated love in her eyes. We were so filled with wonder at our own state of bliss that when we noticed a little caretaker man peeping at us through the banyan limbs, we did not even protest.

Everything was perfect until we went to bed at night.

It's not that it was unexciting. Eugénie was a frenzied, feverish, fearless lover, always interested in novelties. Nothing was off-limits or taboo. She wanted plantains up her pussy. She wanted her ass licked. She wanted to be fucked in a foot of moonless river mud with crocodiles nosing about. She wanted to do it in hotel corridors, the back seats of taxis, outdoor movie theaters, and anywhere else where there was a good chance of getting caught.

God knows, I was no prude. But I just could not get my head around it with Eugénie. Truth is... I was a bit old-fashioned when it came to the woman I wanted to be my wife.

"*One germ inherited from an old love,*" I scribbled in my journal between frantic bouts of lovemaking, "*is enough to infect a new one.*"

In sum, Eugénie was everything I had dreaded all my life, everything I had secretly desired. She thrilled me beyond words yet scared the wits out of me. I wanted romance, but she gave me fever. She tasted better than anything; but she tasted, ultimately, of my own death.

We spent Chinese New Year in Calcutta, awaiting the arrival of our ship to Rangoon, Burma. There was a big party in the dining room of the Southeast Asia Hotel—where we were registered as man and wife—with a local rock band, free Indian food, and an endless supply of champagne. Everyone called us Mr. and Mrs. Brawley, and we were madly in love.

Not knowing how unused to spirits Eugénie was, I let her drink too much champagne. She seemed perfectly normal, having a wonderful time, until it hit her suddenly and she turned into a comic drunk. Burping, hiccupping, she leapt onto the bandstand, elbowed the gaunt little lead guitarist aside, sang a lewd Flemish song off tune, did an outrageous bump and grind, and passed out in my arms.

As I flung her over my shoulder and started up the stairs toward our room, everyone—English, Chinese, and Hindu—stood to cheer.

"Bravo, Mrs. Brawley! Happy New Year!"

The instant we got in the door though, Eugénie vomited all over the bed, then promptly passed out. I bathed her, cleaned up the mess, watched over her, marveling at her Renaissance beauty, the innocence of her breathing, and wondering where she would take me. Then she woke up, still drunk, but in a confessional mood, and told me of all the many men she had fucked in mind-altering detail, including the ones in India that she'd had while I was out of touch: An American hitchhiker very much like me. A handsome hotel clerk. A plump, prosperous Anglo-Indian businessman of sixty-five. A married French couple . . .

"Any sodomy with animals?" I asked. "Any pedophilia? How about necrophilia?"

"Don't be fresh, Ernesto," she replied. "I just want to be open with you."

"Save it for your fellow fucking freaks!" I shouted, and she did not take kindly to that at all.

As we boarded our ship the next morning, the second officer, Lieutenant Picard, a ruggedly handsome Frenchman with a beautifully blond Van Dyke, stood there to greet us. Or rather, he ignored me and saved all his charm for Eugénie.

The *Cambodge* was the flagship of the Méssageries Maritimes Line. *Méssageries* Maritimes was the last company in the world to offer Fourth Class or steerage passage. I was booked in steerage, of course, but Eugénie's father had paid for her passage in First Class. Passengers of the lower orders, like me, were not granted visiting privileges to the other classes on board, but upper-class passengers were permitted to enter steerage anytime they liked. It was four days, however, before Eugénie condescended to grace me with her presence.

"I've got something to tell you," she declared with a grimace when she finally arrived.

"If it's about Yellow Beard, save your breath," I sniffed. "I already guessed."

"You must understand, Ernesto. You hurt me more than anyone ever did before. I am not a freak. I'm free, that's all. Free! What did Anaïs Nin say? *'All but freedom, utter freedom, is death.'* I needed someone mature enough to understand me. You are still an overgrown child, full of absurd romantic notions. With Lieutenant Picard, I felt . . . fulfilled."

After Eugénie had vented her feelings, she abruptly changed her tone. She took my hand, put it on her cheek. Gazing at me soulfully, she said, "Please, Ernesto, don't hate me."

"No, I don't hate you," I said. Yet, at that moment I resolved to bide my time, then give Eugénie what she so obviously wanted and needed.

In Rangoon, we checked into a youth hostel and went out for tea in a little coffee house called "The Muse." With its classical European music playing softly in the background, its wooden floors and walls, windows overlooking the river, the place was quite *gemütlich*. The pine wood of our corner seemed to hold us in, to contain us, as if it were our own squirrels' nest, and all our nuts were gathered within, on that rainy season afternoon. We sipped coffee, drew on our cigarettes, and listened to Rachmaninoff. Music encircled us. The rain outside pressed to get in.

"I love the woody, reedy quality of old Asian buildings, don't you?" I remarked. "The swoosh of stocking feet on polished wooden floors. Doors sliding over straw mats. Everything made of rice paper or straw..."

"Yes," she nodded, "nature is always just around the corner, it seems."

"How do you feel about me now, Eugènie?"

"I still love you," she replied, pausing to draw on her cigarette and blow out the smoke. "But it's remote. I don't need it anymore."

Later we visited the *Shwedagon Pagoda* to sit cross-legged on damp straw. The rain outside tried to get in. Yet, incense filled the air.

Not far from us, a Burmese girl knelt before a large altar, bowing, crying, praying intensely. I could not even begin to imagine what Oriental sorrow possessed her. Probably something to do with a man, I decided.

Eugénie sat cross-legged beside me, her eyes far away, and I felt the weight of the huge temple pillars, each hewn of one gigantic pine tree, all around us. Though the atmosphere inside was frigid, it felt somehow weighty, expectant. The paper windows above us glowed white from the sun behind clouds.

"I thought I was *enceinte*," Eugénie murmured, as we left the temple. "That's why I stayed away from you on the ship. I hated you for getting me that way, for cutting my life short, for chaining me down with your mooning and spooning, your sniffing about."

"And now?" I wondered.

"I don't hate you, Ernesto," she said gaily, lighting up another cigarette. "I just got my period this morning!"

When night fell, we stopped at a noodle shop in Rangoon's Chinatown and had egg drop soup to fortify us against the rain. Later, over some hot *sake*, I pulled out *Proverbs from Hell* by William Blake, which I happened to be reading, and read the following quote to Eugénie.

I read it as if it had just come to me spontaneously, but I had already thought it out very carefully—a fact that did not escape her for an instant:

You never know what is enough
until you know what is more than enough.

She laughed, then pointed to another (apparently contradictory) quote a few pages on in the same book:

The road of excess
leads to the palace of wisdom.

We both had a little giggle about that as well.

Later, walking toward the hostel, we were feeling great, and started capering in the street. I found myself to be tremendously excited, as I often was after this kind of sexual defeat.

We stopped to say goodbye on the corner, and Eugénie looked at me tenderly, but this time I was not going to be seduced.

"Eugènie," I said, breathing deep, "there's something I've wanted to give you for a long time."

"Yes?" she replied, nodding, smiling, as if expecting a gift.

"Something to repay you for everything you've given me, something you really deserve."

"What is it, Ernesto?"

"This!" I roared and slapped her across the face.

Her head snapped back. She staggered with the impact. A patch of bright red spread across her cheek. She shook her head, as if in disbelief.

When at last she opened her eyes—her lovely Flemish Renaissance eyes—I could read pain, bewilderment, and finally understanding there, just as the artist might have painted it.

"Bam!" I shrieked to myself, smacking my fist in my hand as I lay sleepless in the men's dorm that night. "Bam! Did I hit her! Boy, did she deserve it! Bam!"

Curiously, despite our violent parting in Burma, Eugénie and I maintained intermittent contact over the years. I even sent her a copy of my short story "The Fence Between Us," in which she appeared prominently, if not altogether flatteringly.

In the late seventies, when I came through Paris, where Eugénie had settled, we arranged to meet for dinner. Beautiful as ever, she was engaged to a South African diplomat, she said. The wedding was to be in six months, and then she would move with him to Cape Town.

"So," I asked, belligerently, "you've got no objections to marrying a representative of the apartheid regime?"

"*Merde!*" she spat back, "you're not going to get 'holier than thou' on me, are you, Ernesto? After all the scams you pulled?"

"Okay, promise me one thing, then, Eugénie, just for old time's sake."

"What?"

"That you won't name your kids with him either Tristán or Cybèle."

"Oh, have no fear of that!" she scoffed. "How did we ever think of such puerile, jejune appellations, anyway?"

"Fine, whatever you say," I sighed. "Now, what about your career as a pianist?"

"That's over. I work at the South African Embassy now. That's how I met Jan, my fiancé."

"What do you do there?"

"I'm in the Public Relations Department," she said. "I've got English, French and Flemish, which is almost the same as Afrikaans, so I'm really kind of indispensable to them."

"What happened to your other career, your music?"

"You want the truth, Ernesto? I simply wasn't good enough. Do you know what Saint Thomas Aquinas said? *'Only three things are needed for beauty: wholeness, harmony, radiance.'* The consensus seemed to be that I hadn't enough of the latter."

After dinner, I half-expected Eugénie to ditch me, but she wanted to know if I was up for a stroll along the Seine.

Down on the *quai*, on the Île de la Cité, with the river gushing below us, the lights off the *Palais de Justice* playing on its eddying surface, the barges and tourist boats floating by, we mellowed toward each other despite the tension that we had felt all evening. We even walked along hand in hand for a while, just like old times.

Then, almost before either of us realized it—"a quickly extinguished fire is quickly reignited"—we found ourselves pressed up against a stone wall under the *Pont au Change*, kissing feverishly, tearing at each other's clothes, heedless of passersby. I bit her lips, bit her nipples through her blouse. She found bare skin under my shirt, dug into my back with her nails. I pulled my trench coat around us, jerked up her skirt. She dropped her panties round her ankles, slid them off, slipped them into the pocket of her raincoat.

Then right there under the bridge, with gawking pedestrians strolling by, she unbuttoned me, dragged me out into the cold, night air, and plunged me inside her, moaning, crying, and muttering garbled words. Just as I was about to erupt, she yanked me out, fell to her knees, wrapped my trench coat around her head, and blew me as I'd never been blown before, licking the sperm that spouted across her face.

"Oh, I feel so humiliated!" she cried when we were done. Yet, the very next day we were at it again in my hotel.

To make up for the violent passions of the night before, or perhaps as a parting gift to me, Eugénie made love to me sweetly and gently this time, the way I had always wanted.

"The weird thing is, none of it was real, was it?" I observed, as she was leaving.

"*Mait dit donc, Ernesto!*" she cried. "The whole thing was a childish illusion, a passing fancy, a holiday romance. *Le temps des lilas et le temps des roses ne reviendra plus. The time of lilies and roses never returns.*"

"So, what's all this about?" I demanded, jerking my head toward our unmade bed.

"It's about memories," she said, smiling, gazing up at me tenderly, holding my hands in hers. "It's about a fleeting past that we shared. It's about the impermanence of all things. It's about goodbye."

"Yes," I whispered, eyes shut, as I closed the door behind her.

Our feelings had evolved to the point where, for once, and only at our final parting, were we in perfect harmony.

Chapter Fifteen

"Tis better to have loved and lost than never to have loved at all."
Alfred Lord Tennyson.

When I got to Bangkok, alone, I rented a fully furnished two-bedroom luxury apartment on the fourteenth floor of a place called the "Trendy Condominium." My rent—minimal by American standards—included huge wrap-around windows, a terrace, a gorgeous view of Bangkok, maid, linen, and cable service, a sauna, fitness center, and an Olympic size swimming pool.

The Trendy was located on Soi 13 in Sukhumvit, central Bangkok. Sukhumvit was a wealthy yet singularly colorful neighborhood of eccentrically shaped Asian style skyscrapers and narrow teeming lanes clogged with *"farangs"* from every country in the world. There were hippy backpackers fresh off the Great Grass Road, pot-bellied sexual and medical tourists, financial refugees and retirees from Europe, Africa, North and South America, the Middle East, and the Antipodes. The sidewalk markets and outdoor restaurants were choked twenty-four hours a day with spidery, hungry-looking Thai vendors, beggars and bar girls, cheek by jowl with West Africans in national costume, hawk-nosed Arabs in head-dress and full biblical robes, and throngs of hairy red-faced Yanks, Brits, Swedes, Krauts and Aussies in khaki shorts and tank tops imprinted with Singha Beer logos. The crowds of huge, overfed foreigners were predominately old, male, and dour, while their gracile young Thai counterparts were virtually all female and smiling. Aside from the fact that Thailand was "The Land of Smiles," there was a very good reason for this: most male tourists came to Thailand for sexual recreation.

Online dating sites did not exist in the sixties, of course, but the Thais had long before arranged to accommodate their sexual tourists. Immediately upon my arrival in Bangkok, I went to an office with a sign outside that read, "Thai Love Links." A young lady named Pui took down all my personal information, snapped a photo of me, and asked me what type of girl I desired.

"A young, attractive, college-educated, English-speaking girl from a good family," I replied.

"No problem," she said, smiling, nodding. "I have a beautiful, registered nurse with a master's degree available. You will meet her tomorrow at 5:00 p.m. at Wat Suthat Park on Khao San Road."

"How will she know me?"

"Not to worry, dear, I'll tell her what you look like. Okay?"

"Okay," I said, and paid her the required three hundred Thai baht, or nine US dollars.

"And remember," she continued, "everyone here has a code name until they agree to become a couple. Yours will be 'Chuck,' hers will be 'Panda Bear.' Exchange code names when you meet, so there can be no confusion. All right?"

"Fine," I said.

Next day in Wat Suth Park, at exactly 5:00 p.m., a young Thai woman came walking up to me. Slight, dark, and pretty, in a tank top, miniskirt, and high heels, a little sideways grin lit up her face.

"You gotta be Chuck, right?"

"No way to miss me, huh?"

"Not in a million years," she replied and before she finished shaking my hand, she had already won my heart.

"And you gotta be Panda Bear, right?"

"Right! How you guess?"

"Oh, how could I miss such a lovely girl!"

"Flattery will get you everything!" she said, beaming at me. "So, what's your real name, Chuck?"

"Ernesto. What's yours?"

"It's . . . Nana," she replied, a bit shyly, it seemed.

Unlike most Thai ladies, who carry not an ounce of excess body weight, Nana was curvy, voluptuous. As she pranced about the Wat Suthat Park, hips swaying, breasts jiggling, bottom jutting out behind her, the effect was more South American than Asian—and utterly enchanting to my Latin sensibility.

I took her to dinner at the Hotel Thapae on Soi 11, which featured a leafy garden restaurant, an excellent jazz combo, great Thai food, and beautiful, lithe waitresses dressed in traditional Issan garments.

Nana's English was fluent, if a bit ungrammatical. And she was so unabashedly sexy and girly on our first meeting that I expected (and anticipated with pleasure) that she would be the very image of the "Hot Nurse" of my imagination.

To my immense surprise, however, I found very soon that her personality was multi-faceted. Despite her hot-blooded, fun-loving nature, she was neither flighty nor shallow. Indeed, there was something innocent, almost nun-like, in her dark, trusting eyes... and in her bright infectious smile that sometimes turned inward, disappearing in sober reflection.

As it turned out, there was an analytical, intellectual side to Nana's character, and she was amazingly well-read, not just in the medical field. She worked in the Cardiology Clinic at Bumrungrad International Hospital, where she was—I would find out later—a remarkably conscientious nurse, devoted to her patients.

Nana and I had a delightful time that night, devouring barbecued river fish, drinking Australian Chardonnay, laughing, joking, telling our life stories, establishing that we were both single, unattached.

Toward the end of dinner, she leaned across the table, smiled fetchingly, and murmured, "I love to see your place, Ernesto. You live near?"

"Just around the corner," I said, raising a hand to our waiter.

The way it happened was completely natural. We walked into my apartment, and I opened the window to show Nana my spectacular view of nighttime Bangkok. As she leaned out the window, I started sniffing, kissing, biting her soft, fragrant brown neck and shoulders.

With her luscious buttocks thrusting out at me like that, it was impossible to resist the impulse to run my hand up her mini skirt. Then, when goose bumps erupted on her naked shoulders, I dispensed with further preamble. With her head still out the window, she started to moan and wriggle her bottom. And when she came, she squealed her pleasure to the whole, bright, speckled skyline of Bangkok, turning heads on the pool terrace five floors below.

And that was just for starters.

Nana and I were together for two months, without a moment's trouble between us. I gave her a key, and she came over to my place every evening after her shift at the hospital, which was in my Sukhumvit neighborhood. Following a therapeutic after-work quickie, and a swim in my pool, we taxied to a different café or restaurant nearly every night. One night it was Arab food, the next Indian, the next French, then Italian, Japanese, Chinese, Vietnamese. Not to mention the local Thai places which offered our staple fare. Then it was home for a sleepy-time, and a wake-up. Sometimes, there was even an afternoon delight—if Nana had time to pop over to my place during her lunch hour.

Weekends, she left me alone to work for extra pay as a live-in private nurse to an elderly Thai millionaire in Wireless Road.

Or at least that's what I believed until one weekend I heard a knock at my door and opened it to a slender, handsome, Royal Thai Army First Lieutenant wearing a jungle fatigue uniform—including a .45 caliber service pistol in a holster at his waist.

"Good evening, sir," he said, smiling. "I am Lieutenant Nuttakom Methatamsatit. And I have something to say that I believe is of mutual concern. May I come in for a moment?"

I invited him in. And very politely, in perfect, slightly stilted, British English, he informed me that he was Nana's fiancé and had been for the last three years. He was billeted at an army base in Chon Buri, but he had weekends off... all of which he spent at Nana's apartment in Bangkok. Their families approved of their engagement. A traditional dowry sum had already been paid to the father of the bride, and the wedding was set for December.

To prove his assertion and abolish my doubts, Lieutenant Methatamsatit produced from the oversized pocket of his camouflaged bush jacket a series of photos showing him and Nana in various poses over the years—at her graduation from nursing school, at a friend's wedding, on romantic holidays to the islands of Ko Samui and Ko Samet, at their betrothal party with both families in attendance.

"But why?" I asked, gaping at the photos in astonishment. "If this is so, why in the world would she want to be with me?"

At this, Lieutenant Methatamsatit laughed heartily.

"I am afraid, sir, that you do not understand Thai ladies of the middle classes," he said. "They are all very curious by nature, and they like to play, especially with *farangs*. But they marry Thais. It is up to their fiancé or husband to catch them at play and put a stop to it. That is why I am asking you now to kindly cease and desist."

"Have no fear, Lieutenant," I responded, grinning ruefully, shaking my head, eyeing the pistol at his waist. "She's all yours."

"Thank you, sir," he said, smiling back, shaking my hand, turning to go. "And I wish you a happy life."

In the following days, Nana tried to contact me several times by phone, but I refused to answer. She even came to my condo late one night and tried my door with her key, but I had taken the precaution of changing the lock.

"Please, let me just explain!" she sobbed, scratching at the door with her fingernails, but I maintained my silence, and soon I heard her shuffling off down the corridor in her sensible uniform shoes.

After my bitter disappointment with 'Nurse Panda Bear', whom I missed quite desperately for several months, there came a time when I simply indulged my family fever in mindless hanky-panky. Through the offices of Thai Love Links, I met and coupled with several pretty, well-educated ladies from all over the Greater Bangkok area. They rarely lasted over a night or two, and now I can barely recall their names. An accountant, a Yoga teacher, an executive secretary, a pharmacist, a real estate agent, a high school math teacher, none of them held my attention for more than a week. And I learned little about them or their national characteristics, save for one salient fact....

I had all these silly romantic notions when I came to Thailand. From all I'd heard, the Thais were the 20th century equivalent of Rousseau's *Nobel Savage*. But I had been utterly duped. I found that tropical people are just as complex and conniving as their northern counterparts.

Or perhaps even more so.

I went out with all manner of Thai ladies, from the ages of twenty to thirty. None were bar girls or prostitutes. All were college-educated, came from good families, and held respectable jobs. They had only one other thing in common. They each had a sick mother, or a dying father, an overdue car lease, or mortgage, or tuition payment. To put it bluntly, they all—with the unique exception of Nurse Panda Bear—equated love with money.

As a case in point, not long after my break-up with Nana, I met a pretty, thirty-year-old, divorced mother of two. She spoke excellent International School English, had a master's degree in business management, a three-bedroom, two-bathroom house in the suburbs, a brand new Volvo and had until recently been a top manager at a big Japanese firm in Bangkok. I took her to lunch. We had a few drinks and ended up in my condo. We played around a bit but didn't get down to business because she had to leave to get home in time to help the maid make dinner for her kids. The next morning, she phoned me and asked me for the equivalent of $700 for her daughter's fancy, Catholic, school tuition.

"But I barely know you!" I exclaimed. "How can you ask for money?"

She was silent, but the implication was clear. If I wanted more of that tasty stuff that I got a sniff of the afternoon before, I would have to pay through the nose. And the worst of it was—I was sorely tempted.

Then there was the lovely twenty-three-year-old dental assistant who told me that if I wanted to be her "fiancé" I would have to pay her parents 100,000 baht as a "dowry fee."

And the one I invited to go swimming with me in my pool, she said, "Oh, I don't have a swimming suit! But we can zip over to the Emporium and get one." So, we took the Skytrain to the Emporium and she got a modest Thai-style bikini. But she didn't stop there.

She got a miniskirt (in which I admit she looked smashing), a blouse, a couple of pairs of high heeled sandals, and several frilly intimate items.

Afterwards, who got presented with the bill? *Moi!* And the salesgirls looked on in grinning approval as the gullible *farang* forked over his 10,000 baht. But you know what? The oddest thing is, later that night, swimming in my deserted pool in the moonlight, running my hands over that darkly lubricious body, down into that ill-gotten bikini, I believed for a moment or two that it was worth every single baht.

Eventually, I grew tired of the debauchery and petty larceny of Bangkok and decided to take a trip. I traveled by train and bus, *tuk-tuk* and motorbike, mule, and foot, all through Thailand and Laos. I trekked through the mountains, visiting the Long Neck People, the Long Ear People, the Tin Head People, the River Gypsies (the descriptive phrases remarkably apt), smoking opium in a long-stemmed pipe with the Lost Opium Army of the Kuomintang Chinese. I rode the bucking Mekong in a long-tailed boat and rafted down the sluggish River Maenamsae to the villages of the Giant Snake People and the Wild Elephant People.

I rented a big, fast, 650 cc. Kawasaki motorcycle—despite a premonition that it might not turn out for the best—and explored the hinterlands of the Issan Region of Northeastern Thailand, along the Laotian border, called "The Golden Triangle," visiting the exotic cities of Nong Khai, Beung Kan, and Nakhon Phanom.

Before leaving each town, I made it a point to stop at the local office of the nationwide Thai Love Links network, where I would set up a date with a lady in the next town on my route. In this way, I came into romantic contact with the mysterious, gold-digging beauties Tien, Nui, Jiab, and Mem, whose stories—interesting though they may be—pale beside the one that I am about to recount.

In Nakhon Phanom, I arranged a luncheon date with a lady named Pang—a twenty-six-year-old high school librarian—in Mukdahan, the next city on my route through the Issan area. Mukdahan is a nondescript market town located just across the mile-wide Mekong from a thriving Laotian city called Savannakhet.

Though Mukdahan is not the most interesting town in Thailand, it would forever be engraved in my memory.

Arriving there at noon, I checked into a cheap but clean hotel on the river promenade, next door to the Indochina Night Market, both of which came highly recommended by my road bible, *Lonely Planet*. I took a cold shower, changed clothes, headed downstairs, cranked up my bike, clapped on my helmet, and set out for my luncheon date.

As it turned out, Ms. Pang lived a bit out of town, on the river road that led to Mukdahan National Park. We were to meet just across the street from her place in what *Lonely Planet* called "a charming floating restaurant with an intriguing name: *Wine Wild Why?*"

Unfortunately, however, I was destined to taste neither the delights of *Wine Wild Why?* nor those of Ms. Pang because The Living Buddha—forever inscrutable—had arranged that I meet my fate before I reached there.

I was heading down the highway—driving on the left-hand side of the road according to a Thai law that is largely ignored in rural areas—with the Mekong River on my left, rice fields, and long-horned water buffalos on my right. The sun was out, but it was refreshingly cool.

The wind on my face felt sweetly humid. As always, I was thrilled, energized by the speed of my bike, the sound of its exhaust, and of the exotic place—a world away from Chino, California—where I found myself now. Not to mention my coming date with the tantalizing Ms. Pang, whose sensual Thai Love Links profile photo—with just a tip of pink tongue peeping from a corner of her mouth—I had indelibly imprinted in my memory.

So, there I was, happy as a clam, growling along on my bike at 50 mph, when suddenly this big, six-wheeled truck and trailer with a load of sugar cane overtook me on the right like I was standing still. I could see two men in it, both dark, peasant-looking, one of them old and thin, the other young and fat. They were passing a bottle of Thai whiskey back and forth, tipping it up, laughing uproariously.

Immediately, I was on my guard, ready for anything. Thank the Lord Buddha I was, for suddenly the thin old man in the truck frantically signaled the fat young driver to turn left. Without a glance behind, he slammed on his brakes, cutting right in front of me—his load teetering precariously—aiming for a dirt side road that led down to a riverside dock.

I had only an instant to decide my fate, for the truck and trailer were immediately in front of me, at a right angle to the path of my motorcycle, and the distance between us was closing at lightning speed.

I had two choices, neither of which seemed very appetizing. One was to crash into the side of the trailer at 50 mph, possibly decapitating myself. The other was to hit the asphalt and hope to slide either under the trailer or around its rear end. Instinctively choosing the latter option, I turned my front wheel sharply right and crammed on my rear brake, which instantly swung my rear wheel around and brought me down hard.

My right shoulder and helmet struck the pavement with an audible FLUMP. But I felt nothing. And I was still conscious enough to try and get my right leg out from under the motorcycle. The problem was that the bike had slammed down too suddenly for me to react in time, so my leg stayed pinned beneath its full weight as it slewed across the rough surface of the highway.

I slid for fifty feet or more, missing the rear wheels of the truck.

All the time I was skidding across the blacktop—frying my right leg against the hot engine on one side, ripping it to the bone on the other—I had only one thing in mind.

It was not fear of death.

It was a dream sequence from many years before... a remarkably similar scene in which I was sliding across the asphalt in front of Suzanne Mutaberria's house on Riverside Drive, scraping skin to the bone, scattering *Pomona Progress-Bulletins* all over the highway.

In nearly two decades, I had not learned a thing.

Still out there on the fever road, to my own mortal peril.

At some point the bike and I parted ways, and we ended up on the side of the road about twenty feet apart. By the time I came to my senses in a pile of water buffalo shit, the truck had disappeared down the dirt road to the river. But a solicitous crowd of Thai peasants—some wearing the emblematic black pajamas and conical straw hats of the borderland—had gathered around me. From whence they came, I had no idea. Jabbering in their guttural Issan dialect (an archaic form of Laotian), they made sympathetic noises, dabbed at my weeping wounds with toilet paper and dirty hankies.

It took me a moment, but at last I was able to assess my situation. I had suffered a compound fracture of my right ankle and leg. This was clear because two bloody bones were sticking out of them. My right shoulder was dislocated, and I could not move my right arm. I was suffering from deep lacerations and abrasions, all of which were embedded with road grit and buffalo shit. Fortunately, my head seemed to have suffered no serious damage, and I found myself to be strangely calm for someone in my predicament.

In fact, I found that I was so self-possessed that while still lying in the road I could gesture to the eldest of the peasants, indicating that I needed to be carried to a telephone booth. As it happened, there was a grocery store with a telephone only a few yards away, and its kindly proprietor phoned for an ambulance immediately. Then I asked with a hand gesture if I might use his phone, to which he replied with a smile and nod.

My first call was to Ms. Pang. Due to a traffic accident, I informed her that I would be unable to make our luncheon date. I made no demands on her, and she seemed relieved that I did not, especially when I described my current physical condition. She seemed rather wary of me now, as if I'd suddenly acquired such horrifically bad karma that it might somehow rub off on her.

My second call was to Nurse Panda Bear, whom I hadn't spoken to in months. Since she was the only qualified medical professional I knew in Thailand, I phoned her as an emergency measure, merely to seek advice. Fortunately, she was working night shifts at her hospital, so she was available to talk. After getting over her initial shock at hearing from me after all this time, and in such grave circumstances, she seemed quite concerned about me and had me go over my symptoms in some detail.

"Okay, Ernesto," she said, suddenly all business. "Have an ambulance take you to the Mukdahan branch of Bumrungrad Hospital. Only good one in town, *na*? I will take a few days off—I have some time coming—and I'll be there tomorrow morning."

"But Nana, you're too kind. You don't have to do that. I mean . . ."

"You crazy? You *tingtong*? Your condition is serious. You will need me, for sure. Anyway, my friend Mimi from nursing school, she works there. Be nice to see her again, *na?*"

The ambulance arrived, siren blaring, and I had to ring off. The paramedics lifted me onto a stretcher and carried me aboard. One of them asked a young rice farmer in knee boots if he would ride my bike into the hospital and leave it in the parking lot. Everyone was sincerely concerned about me, and eager to help. I was so overwhelmed by their instinctive kindness that I almost cried but managed to smile at them in appreciation. They all grinned back, showing big rows of red betel-stained teeth, and flashed me the V sign, still jabbering at me in their incomprehensible dialect.

In the hospital, I was rushed into the operating room (in Thailand a "rush" often lasts two or three hours).

After I'd been properly anesthetized, and my wounds had been cleaned and disinfected, a cheerful and competent young surgeon set my bones, attached them with steel plates and screws, sewed up my surgical incisions and other lesions, bound them with bandages, and placed a removable cast on my leg.

It was a long, tedious process, lasting most of the afternoon and evening. But I didn't feel anything. In fact, I was so cheerful and light-headed from painkillers that I cracked jokes with the attending staff all the way through the procedure. Afterwards, they hit me with some kind of intravenous knockout drop, and I didn't know a thing till the next day.

I woke up in a clean, sunny, hospital room full of tropical flowers, with a young Thai nurse leaning over me, smiling sweetly, making little cooing noises.

Nurse Panda Bear!

"You okay, darling?" she asked.

"Am I okay?" I laughed. "I must've died and gone to heaven!"

"I looked through your clothes, found receipts. Checked you out of your hotel room. Brought all your stuff here. And I phoned the motorcycle shop. A man will come get it. You must pay for damage."

"You're an angel, Nana."

"Nothing to it," she said, cracking her little sideways grin. "You know, I still got a special feeling for you, Ernesto."

For five days, Nurse Panda Bear attended to me personally, sleeping in my room, feeding me, cleaning my wounds, changing my bandages and washing my body by hand. When she needed to rest for a moment, her smiley friend, Nurse Mimi, took over. Rules were so lax at the hospital that Nana could even creep into my bed at night and minister to my sexual needs. Her nursing skills were so expert that she could manage it without popping a single stitch.

"But what about your fiancé?" I inquired, after one particularly memorable midnight encounter.

"Hey, this is a medical emergency!" said Nana, laughing delightedly. "Not his business. Anyway, I am sick of that man. Always creeping around, checking on me. Like a private dick, *na*? How can I marry a man like that?"

"Haven't the foggiest."

"Why do you think I got my thing with you, Ernesto?"

"I'm clueless."

"Trying to get away from *him!* But then, you see, I really *fell* for you, *na?*"

"You still feel that way about me?" I marveled.

"Uh-huh," she said, smiling, nodding.

"You sure you about that?"

"Yes, yes, yes!"

"I can't imagine why!" I replied, laughing.

"Why? I don't know either. Haha! Must be crazy. *Tingtong!*"

"How's your fiancé going to feel when he finds out we're together again?"

"Not so good. But you know what? He just gonna have to get used to it."

"Somehow I can't see him doing that."

"Hey!" she burst out. "He don't own me, right?"

"Right," I agreed, yet I was still not as sanguine about the prospect as Nana seemed to be.

When the doctor declared that I was ready to travel, Nana checked me out of the hospital, put me in a taxi, supervised my boarding of the train in a wheelchair, and held my hand all the way back to Bangkok. I was so perfectly content that I forgot about her pistol-packing fiancé for the entire trip.

When we rolled into Bangkok Station, I pulled Nana up close by the chin, gazed into her big, dark, up-slanted eyes, and whispered to her, "Nana, I owe you, my life."

"Uh-huh," she laughed. "And pretty soon you gonna have to pay, *na?*"

"What?"

"Ha ha! Look at your face. Just kidding, Ernesto! Just kidding. *Tingtong*!"

In Bangkok, Nana moved into my condo again and nursed me through the entire two months of my convalescence. Through some miracle of persuasion, she managed to break off her engagement, convincing her heartbroken fiancé and their two families that they had outgrown each other, and that she had to "move on to new life."

I had no precise idea how she accomplished it, but the ease of her escape could perhaps be attributed to the fact that she told her parents and fiancé nothing of her renewed relationship with me and swore to them all in the name of Lord Buddha that no other man had taken his place in her heart. When the lieutenant asked where she spent her time when not at the hospital, she told him what she had once told me in a similar situation: she had taken on an extra job as private nurse to an elderly gentleman.

Nevertheless, I was still highly skeptical. The lieutenant with the unpronounceable name that I had met was neither as credulous nor as naïve as Nana now painted him. But I was so preoccupied with my recovery and physical rehabilitation— and so blissful with dear Nurse Panda Bear—that I set all my misgivings aside.

Even when the lieutenant mailed me to say he'd heard all about Nana and me and threatened to break my other leg, I accepted her unsupported opinion that these were merely idle threats. Thanks to Nana's continuing reassurances, I maintained my (uneasy) calm even when we spotted him lurking outside my condo one night in his civilian clothes, even after he accosted her in the lobby of her hospital and had to be escorted from the premises by security officers.

With Nurse Panda Bear's devoted care, my recovery was nothing short of amazing. It was not long before I was swimming in my condo's pool every day, hopping all over my neighborhood.

As for our personal relations, we got along even better than the last time around. And our sex life was every young man's wet dream.

We planned a big, local wedding where I would dress up like Yul Brynner and Nana like a Thai princess in *The King and I*. After which, I would secure her a marriage visa to the USA, and we would move to Los Angeles, where she would take a state test to become a registered nurse, get a job at a local hospital, and—as she said—"make big American money."

Then, just three days before our wedding, wouldn't you know?

Lieutenant Nuttakom Methatamsatit showed up at my door while Nana was at work. He had three fully armed military police officers with him, and a court order to have me deported immediately as an "undesirable alien." When I objected, the lieutenant ordered one of the military policemen to handcuff me and escort me downstairs to a paddy wagon waiting in the street. I was then conducted directly to Bangkok International Airport, where I was forced onto a jet bound for Tokyo.

The last thing I saw before the plane took off was Lieutenant Nuttakom Methatamsatit laughing and slapping hands with his military policemen buddies on the runway.

The sad part was this: I tried to reach Nurse Panda Bear for weeks after that, by phone, letter, and telegram, but I never heard from her again. I assumed she had been roped into marriage with the lieutenant, but I had no way of knowing for sure, and it took me years to get over her.

Chapter Sixteen

*Blossoms are scattered by the wind
and the wind cares nothing,
but the blossoms of the heart
no wind can touch.*

Yoshida Kenko, 1330

When I arrived in Tokyo, virtually penniless, I happened to meet an American expatriate, a fellow Californian named Bob Newburgh, in a bar called *Fugetsu-do*, frequented by young foreigners. Though he found my story of "love lost" most amusing, he sympathized with my predicament.

As it happened, Bob worked for an American-owned film distribution company, and within a week he had secured me a well-paying job as a movie extra at Toho Co., Ltd., Japan's largest film company. So, for the next few months, any time a young, white face was needed in a film, I was it!

Yes, I know. Yet another rags to riches story!

I spent almost a year in Japan, having lots of fun, visiting every island, every art museum in Tokyo... classical Japanese art is my absolute favorite in the world!

Just before I left, I went on a farewell excursion with my Tokyo girlfriend, a delicate, porcelain creature named Masako Okamura, whom I'd met on the set of a television series called *Ultraman*.

Accompanied by a group of rapt, religious *Shinto* tourists, we sailed to the sacred island of Miajima in the Inland Sea, where there is a famous shrine and an equally famous troop of tame apes.

Although Masako was a talented aspiring actor, she was afflicted with an extreme form of Asian diffidence. Shy and self-effacing, she was petrified of "standing out" or causing a spectacle of any kind.

Moreover, she was acutely sensitive to the fact that she was dating an outlander, a *gaijin*, which might provoke censure among her compatriots.

To add to Masako's discomfort, she had learned over the months that her paramour, Ernesto, was burdened with two distinct but contrasting personalities. One was a reflective, artistic intellectual. The other was a loud-mouthed show-off—a tease.

Indeed, he once confessed to her in a rare candid moment that for as long as he could remember his tranquil, soulful self—what he called *"Ernesto el Bueno"*—had conflicted with his crass, soulless self—*Ernesto el Malo."* Unfortunately, he admitted, because of his family's 'hereditary fever,' the efforts of *el Bueno* had been largely unsuccessful. The result being that *el Malo* remained ascendant.

And nothing in the world set off *el Malo* like the coyness, the timidity of an Asian woman.

For this reason, Masako was horrified, but not particularly astonished, when on their last outing together—her lover perversely conceived a plan to bring about what she most feared, and to taunt her past endurance.

"*Masako-san*?" I said, as we climbed the spiraling trail toward the shrine. "Did you know that in English a synonym for the verb 'to imitate' is the verb 'to ape'? The reason for this is that apes will copy whatever you do. *Wakatta desuka*?"

"*Nanchate, erunesto-san!*" Masako warned in the soft, breathy, confidential tone that she reserved for my most profound cultural transgressions. "You are kidding, Mr. Ernesto, you are kidding, of course!"

"Not at all," I replied, as we reached the mountaintop, ignoring her veiled, reproachful look. "Just watch!"

I swaggered over to where the middle-aged Japanese tourists, each sporting a little, white, sun hat, were snapping pictures in front of the shrine while feeding peanuts to a great, bearded, male ape who seemed to be the leader of the tribe.

I approached the ape, then stuck out my tongue. The ape grinned and followed suit. I thrust my thumbs into my ears while wriggling my fingers at him, which he copied to perfection. I flapped my elbows like a bird, which the ape did as well. I jumped in the air, spun around, and landed just as I was. The ape did that too.

By then, all the Japanese tourists were slapping their thighs in glee, snapping pictures like mad, while Masako was hanging back near the pinewood, trying to pretend that she had never seen this *henna gaijin,* this crazy foreigner, in her life.

Finally, as my *pièce de résistance,* I put up my dukes, beat my chest like Tarzan, and issued the ape a noisy invitation to a boxing match.

The ape put up his dukes as well, then beat his chest. For a moment it looked like he might just go a round or two with me, Marquis of Queensberry Rules, when suddenly he reverted to his animal instincts. Howling in fury, he leapt upon me, wrapped his claws around my throat, and started taking ferocious bites out of the collar of my down coat.

Now I was no longer laughing or joking, but screaming in terror, which made the Japanese tourists guffaw even more. They crowded each other to get shots of this unprecedented spectacle of the *bakka hakujin,* the stupid white man, and the ape.

But I could not care less, for now I was in a shitstorm of trouble. Spinning on heel, I tore off down the winding trail to the ferryboat like a dog with its tail on fire, with the fierce brown ape—whooping in victory—hot on my ass.

Later, safe on the ferryboat by some miracle, I expected Masako to ignore me, to pretend she had never met this *hakujin* in her life, but she astonished me with an almost motherly solicitude.

"But why? Why would you ever do such a thing?" she kept marveling, as she bathed my wounds in the ladies' restroom and bound them with material from the boat's first aid kit. "*Anataga wakaranai.* I understand nothing about you."

"For the fun of it," I replied in English. But it was *Ernesto el Malo* still talking, trying for bravado, but not quite making it.

We took the train to Yokohama, where I had stowed my gear, and where my ship, the *Arlanza*, a Hong Kong-based tramp of British registration, awaited me.

There were storms all the way, while tears pearled up in the corners of Masako's dark eyes and curled down her ivory face like the rain on my window.

After we had kissed and said our final *sayonaras* amid a crowd of British sailors and their weeping bargirls on the windswept Yokohama docks, after I had turned and started for the gangway ladder, Masako forgot her native timidity for an instant.

"*Hajioshire, erunesto-san! Hajioshire! Orokamono!*" she shrieked at my retreating back. "Shame on you, Mr. Ernesto! Shame on you! You are such a foolish man!"

What she meant by that, I hadn't a clue.

As we cleared the dock. I stood on the stern with the sailors, waving into the driving rain.

We pulled out into choppy, squally Tokyo Bay, while Masako and the other little *nihonjin* girls were still waving at us from under their colorful Japanese umbrellas, getting smaller and smaller.

Finally, they disappeared altogether.

I borrowed a pair of binoculars to focus on the dock. All the girls had gone but one.

Though I was invisible to her now, Masako kept waving at me frantically, as if we were still within eye contact.

She was waving a long, linen handkerchief that I had bought for her only the day before, in a handicraft shop near the Kobe railway station, on our way back from the island of Miajima.

It was white, with small, green, hand-painted monkeys on it. Some held their hands over their eyes. Others held them over their ears, others over their mouths.

"Arigato gonzai masu," Masako had said, when I got it for her. "I like it very much, *erunesto-san*. But why this one in particular?"

"Doitashimashite," I replied. "Because you were born in the Year of the Monkey, and I hope it will bring you luck."

"Somehow, I'm not quite sure that's the only reason," she said. "I think perhaps it's some kind of message to me."

"It is what it is," I responded in English, but Masako had me figured.

There was even more to it than she guessed though, for my imagination has always been held perversely in thrall to the three giant mastiff dogs, *Ciego*, *Sordo* and *Mudo*, or Blind, Deaf and Dumb, that guarded my Uncle Tom's mortuary and seraglio in Chino, California.

A week later, when my ship docked in Nakhodka, Russia, the civilian port for Vladivostok, I reached into the bottom of my rucksack for a sweater and found an envelope that Masako must have put there sometime before I left Japan.

Inside, on a folded piece of fine paper, there were two short poems written in her elegant calligraphy.

The first one was entitled "*Erunesto-san*," and it can be translated as follows:

I am me!
says the raindrop
as he falls
upon the sea.

The second was entitled "*Masako-san*," and I have translated it thus:

In the other room
Through the wall
Rodents move . . .
I'm not alone after all.

Two years later, at an art house on Clay Street in San Francisco, I caught sight of Masako again, in an obscure, inept samurai film in which she was the only thing of beauty.

Wondering how I could have ever left anyone so impossibly lovely, so impossibly fine, I looked for Masako after that, in every Japanese film that came out, but I never saw her again.

Thirty years later, a young foreign graduate student named Miki Okamura enrolled in one of my writing courses at Hunter College in New York.

"I know that Okamura is a common name in Japan," I said to her, on the first day of class. "But I notice that you're from Nagi, in Yamaguchi Prefecture, which is a very small town. So, I'll ask anyway. Are you in any way related to an actor from the sixties named Masako Okamura? She was born and raised in Nagi."

"Well, yes, Professor; such a coincidence," she replied, raising an eyebrow, a bit suspiciously, it seemed. "Second sister of my father. How do you know her?"

"We worked on a TV film together when I lived in Tokyo. How's she doing?"

"She died when she was very young. About 1970, I think."

"I'm so sorry to hear that," I said, my voice trembling. "If you don't mind my asking, how did she die?"

"Suicide, my father said."

"Oh, my God!"

"God, He's got nothing to do with it, Professor. She jumped in front of a train in Shimbashi Station."

"But why?" I cried out. "Why would she ever do such a thing? She was so young, so beautiful, so talented!"

"Unhappy in love," they say. "*Gaijin, amerikajin*, he ran away and left her alone. You are not the one, I hope."

"I—I pray not," I responded, but my answer did not seem to satisfy her, and she dropped my class the next day.

Chapter Seventeen

One fire burns out another's burning.
WILLIAM SHAKESPEARE, 1594

After an endless trip across Soviet Russia on the Trans-Siberian Railway, I fetched up in Helsinki, Finland, without a kopek.

Flogging my winter coat in the flea market on the quay, I started hitchhiking around the Gulf of Bothnia in a light, woolen sweater, and a hooded rain slicker. But auto-stop in Scandinavia is chancy at best. The weather in August is often more like autumn than summer. The Nords themselves are not notable for their solicitude toward shaggy, itinerant, young strangers. So, there were several times when it was touch and go. In Turku, I broke into a university dormitory to spend the night in a tubful of hot water. On the Swedish border, I got caught in a severe windstorm, spent the night running up and down the empty highway, waving my arms, beating my chest, shouting into the forest to stave off the cold. In Stockholm, I rolled out my sleeping bag in a city park that turned out to be infested with middle-aged pederasts.

The whole way, I ate nothing but handouts and amphetamine tabs.

By the time I hit the Norwegian frontier, I was seeing things: giant white marmots in the roadway, white bats swirling about the car, white mice running up and down my sleeves, ghostly white faces from my past.

Then in Bergen, after a couple of nights in jail (broke a store window to get arrested and out of the cold) I got lucky. A Panamanian sailor I met in a waterfront bar steered me to the *Balboa Trader*, and I signed on as an unpaid work-your-way hand an hour before she was to sail for New York.

After ten stormy days at sea, I landed at Pier Six nearly penniless, and still three thousand miles from home.

Whereupon I promptly got mugged.

Luckily, my sole friend in New York, Misty Thorssen, happened to live only a few blocks away on Charles Street in Greenwich Village.

Her street was narrow and cobbled, I found, with tall shade trees, buckling sidewalks, and fancy grillwork on the fire escapes and stoops. In the pale light of a damp morning in August, it seemed charming, almost picturesque.

Misty had described her place to me as a basement apartment in an old, five story, red brick building, and I found it easily. The only red brick building on the block, it was just across from a row of elegant brownstones with tall narrow windows and carved wooden doors.

Plucking a white rose from the bush beside her stoop, I stepped down a flight of mossy, crumbling brick stairs, swung my backpack off my shoulder, punched her buzzer, then waited, praying she would be home.

Hoping for maybe a touch as well.

A night's lodging.

Greyhound fare to the Coast.

Yet, I was not particularly surprised when no one answered. The address was weeks old, and Misty had never been one to let grass grow under her feet.

I even had a flash that she might be dead, like several other people I knew on the road.

Heaving the rucksack on my shoulder again, turning to go, I glanced at the front window, noticed a crack in the straw curtain, and could not resist a peek inside.

Adjusting my eyes to the light, I saw a long, narrow three-room railroad flat that ran all the way to the other end of the building. Bookshelves and posters advertising contemporary art shows crowded the exposed brick walls. Futons and large, fluffy pillows lay about the straw-matted floor. Indian bedspreads adorned the ceiling, the beds, and what remained of wall space. Big potted coleus plants dangled in the windows.

Peering in at that leafy wonderland of bohemian domesticity, yearning to be let in, I allowed my mind to wander to the farthest, furriest edges of possibility.

The last time I had seen Misty was on board the good ship *Sabarmati*, on its crossing from the port of Karachi to the Rann of Kutch. Though her Afghan hash had obscured my memory of most of the voyage, I did recall with absolute clarity the first few hours that we were aboard. A troupe of fancifully attired Gujarati Gypsies got up to sing and dance wildly and wonderfully about the deck. Then quite suddenly, before they could even pass the hat, they all fell seasick at once, dropped to the deck in a great pile of arms and legs, and fainted away on their own vomit.

Nor will I soon forget the raging squall that came up out of nowhere to cleanse the deck and drive the sub-continentals below, leaving Misty and me alone on the aft cargo hatch when the moon emerged yellow and dripping, like a ghost of Lord Jim, from the Arabian Sea.

Then—something I never divulged to Eugènie, my love interest of the time—Misty and I fell under the spell of that moon. Tearing madly at each other, we rolled off the hatch and onto the slippery wooden deck while the wind blew, the spray flew and the creaking old Conradian steamer heaved, lunged, and fell away beneath us.

Afterwards, lying entwined with her on the wooden deck, drenched in sweat, seawater, and sexual secretions, I grew suddenly, feverishly, tumescent again. Yet, as soon as Misty perceived the direction of my thoughts, she leapt up, I recall—statuesque in the moonlight, a halo of salt spray round her golden crown—and said, "I'm sorry, but that's it, 'Nesto."

"Aw, come on, Misty..."

"Never take a good thing too far, boy," she said, flinging me off, moving around the bulkhead, down the stairway, laughing tauntingly. "Always leave yourself wanting a little more..."

I never ran into Misty again, after I disembarked in India. Barely even heard from her, except for a card now and then, via

American Express, from some exotic locale. Her last note came from this same address:

> *Happy to say I've finally cleaned up my act, gotten myself into drug rehab and settled in.*

"The fuck you looking at?" a female voice blared from behind the door.

"Uh, looking for Misty," I said, jumping in fright. "She in?"

"Who's asking?"

"Ernesto," I replied. "A friend."

"Ernesto? 'Nesto? Is it really you?"

The door flew open and there she was, Misty herself, bigger than life: six feet tall in her bare feet, wearing a red, silk, Chinese dressing gown with a green and blue peacock design, long hoop earrings, an African trade-bead necklace, jangling silver bracelets. Her full-lipped, sharply chiseled, Minnesota-Swedish face was deeply tanned, as if she'd just returned from a month in Guadeloupe. Her yellow-blue eyes, her wild Pre-Raphaelite hair, shone like gold.

"M-Misty," I stammered, gaping at her in wonder. "I . . . uh, just got in from Bergen, Norway, last night. Got mugged as soon as I stepped off the boat."

"Poor baby," she cooed, shaking her head, smiling. "Still out there kicking up dust, huh?"

"Yeah, it's come to the point where I'm lugging around nothing but a load of travel journals," I said. "They've crowded out all but my toothbrush. Anyone with an ounce of common sense would just chuck 'em all, right? But I can't bring myself to do it."

"No difference between *'the thing and its meaning,'* huh?"

"Uh-huh, but you know what, Misty. Sometimes, I think, after a few years on the road the exotic thing is a wife and kids, a straight job, a house, a mortgage, and a car. You dig what I mean?"

"Don't make me laugh!" she retorted, but then proceeded to do just that, throwing her head back to show her long, sharp, white teeth.

"Yeah, well other times it's just the opposite," I observed. "Right? Like, this one night down in Rio de Janeiro? I dropped my ruck and clothes on the beach at Copacabana to go for a swim. When I got back, someone had swiped it all, including my passport. Anyone else would have freaked, right? Naked, penniless, alone in that huge foreign city? But me? I just raised my hands toward the sea and screamed, "Hey, there's nowhere but up from here, baby!"

"Another of your tales, 'Nesto," Misty scoffed, shaking her head. "I don't know how much you make up, but I must admit they're all entertaining. So come on in, sweetie. The least I can do is offer you a cup of coffee."

Hefting the backpack from my shoulders, Misty saw me in, lit some incense, seated me on a large, yellow, Indian pillow, and put "White Rabbit" on the stereo. She retired to the kitchen for a moment, brought out a plate full of Danish and a couple of hand-turned ceramic mugs full of steaming *café-au-lait,* then set them down on her low cable spool coffee table.

"Wow!" I exclaimed, lounging back on a pile of Indian pillows. "This can't be real."

"You're right," she snickered. "Gotta go to work in a minute or two."

"Mind if I stick around?"

"Be my guest, dude! Use the bath if you feel like it. There's a *jelaba* in the closet. Fits all sizes. I'll be back this evening sometime."

Taking Misty's advice, I curled up on one of the futons. Didn't know a thing till she walked in that night.

"Now, where were we, Ernesto?" she asked, slipping behind the closet door, stepping out of her clothes and into her kimono again, placing "Ruby Tuesday" on the stereo.

"I was about to catch you up on my most recent adventures," I reminded her.

Folding her long, long legs, Misty sat down beside me on the futon, produced a vial of cocaine and poured out a couple of lines on a piece of red wrapping paper.

"Hey, I thought you said you were cured of that shit!" I teased.

"Guess I had some kind of . . . relapse," she sighed.

"Mmmmm, well lemme see," I said, accepting her rolled hundred-dollar bill, snorting deep, long, feeling my heart take off like a quail. "A month ago, I found myself in Tokyo. I had a four-tatami room in Shinjuku, and a pretty girlfriend named Masako, but the winter had been long, and . . ."

"Oh, 'Nesto, what a wonderful liar you are!" Misty tittered when I was done recounting my adventures. Yet there was an expression of warmth and affection on her handsome strong-jawed face that was unfamiliar to me.

"It's God's truth, I swear."

"Of course it is. Come here, sweetie, give us a kiss. . . ."

She would not let me do anything. Pushed me down on the purple coverlet, ran a hand up under the *jelaba*, worked at me till I grew big in her palm. Then flung a leg across and settled with a sigh, her kimono hiked up over her broad, tan-lined hips.

Later, she put on "Strawberry Fields Forever," laid out another line, stripped me to the skin, and anointed me with olive oil. Smelling like tossed salad, slippery as eels, we rocked and rolled on her *tatami* mat till we looked like straw dummies.

Later still, after a lingering bath, we made love tenderly to Van Morrison's "Brown-Eyed Girl," my favorite song, and I broke down in tears.

"The fuck you bawling for, 'Nesto?" Misty fumed. "Just a while ago you were full of beans."

"I don't know, I don't know!" I sobbed. "For joy, for sadness, for all the things I've . . ."

"I'm sorry, man," she whispered, shaking her head, and I felt her go stiff beside me on the bed, "but I just can't deal with that kind of shit right now. You know? That kind of *need*. Got way too much on my plate."

Misty asked nothing of me after that, made no demands. She even cut my hair, shaved my beard, gave me some clean clothes to wear (a tee shirt, sweatshirt, Levis and sneakers which had belonged to some previous lover), let me sleep on the futon across the room. Yet, she kept the refrigerator bare, and most of the time I was left entirely to my own devices.

After Misty went out each day, I lingered in the apartment for hours, watering her plants, feeding her tropical fish. Later, I pattered barefoot out to her tiny, overgrown, back garden where I reclined on a rusty, mildewed, lounge chair to read her *High Times* magazines, her books on astrology, the occult, obscure Eastern religions:

> TRANSCENDENT TRUTH
> CANNOT BE REVEALED
> TO ANYONE WHO HAS NOT
> GAINED THE SELF-EXPERIENCE
> OF GOD BECOMING MANIFEST IN MAN

I listened to the IRT subway trains rumble by under Seventh Avenue. Smoked stale cigarettes that I found in odd crannies around the apartment. Drank gallons of water from her garden hose to stave off the hunger pangs.

A couple of times a day, the phone rang, and I would answer it. Sometimes, I was asked to relay messages to Misty in the cryptic jargon of the drug trade, from someone called Al, someone called Ray whose voice sounded familiar.

Eventually, though, hunger would drive me into the streets. I did not have a key, so once I was out, I had to stay out until Misty got home. Most nights, she came in late. Sometimes, she didn't return until three or four o'clock in the morning. On weekends, she didn't come home at all.

I could have sneaked on the subway and ridden up to George Washington Bridge. Could have hiked across to the Jersey side and stuck out my thumb. Might have gotten a ride with a traveling salesman, or a long-haul truck, all the way out to the Golden State.

But Misty... Misty had milked me of my will.

I could have phoned my father collect, asking for enough money to get me home. And there were times I was tempted. Yet, when I thought of our harsh parting words, when I ran out on his beloved California State Department of Corrections without giving notice, I figured it would cost me more in pride than it was worth.

So, for days and nights I wandered the Village, ransacking garbage bins for refundable bottles, hawking stolen newspapers, begging in the subway, sleeping in train stations, dreaming of a soft bed, patiently awaiting Misty's return.

One night, plopping down Jane Street in the rain, I spied a short, muscular Hispanic boy in white sneakers leap to the trailing end of a fire escape ladder, catch it, swing up like a trapeze artist, climb the steps, then disappear into an unlit window on the second floor.

It was such an amazing performance, and it happened so fast—in a blink or two of an eye—that it occurred to me I might do something of the same. In college, I'd done some rock climbing. I was still nimble, light on my feet. It'd be a cinch. I could crawl up Misty's fire escape to the roof, run across to the rear, slide down the rain drainpipe, break into her apartment through the back window.

Still, when it came right down to it, I just couldn't do it. Misty might get pissed, I thought, and throw me out on my ass.

Locked out again on another long, cold, rainy weekend night, I found a battered Volkswagen bus on Hudson Street with its rear door unlocked. Checking to make sure no one was looking, I heaved it open, crawled in, slammed it behind me.

Inside, it was musty, humid, smelling of sex. I rolled up in an old blanket; and in no time my wet clothes were warm and sweaty. The windows of the bus steamed up, cutting the streetlight. The atmosphere turned hot and close. My shivering stopped. Toward morning, despite the persistent itch of the woolen blanket against the exposed portions of my skin, I finally got some sleep.

"Hushaby," said the master. "*Lullaby. Die, dog. Little dog die.*"

A couple of days later, sitting at the end of an abandoned pier at the foot of Little West Twelfth Street, I felt myself starting to itch again. All up and down my crotch, my ass, under my arms, my skin was on fire. I swung down under the pier, then stood on the black scummy rocks to piss in the cold green waters of the Hudson. Peeling my trousers down, examining myself in the harsh sunlight, I found a myriad of tiny white crab-lice eggs clustered at the roots of my pubic hair.

From years of experience—in India, I'd once had such a virulent strain that it kept spontaneously generating for months—I knew the exact prescription: *Wash and dry all clothes and bedclothes at high temperature, shave pubic hair, generously apply Pyrinate 200 lotion to roots.* Trouble was—the laundromat and the treatments were going to cost a lot more than I could make hawking stolen newspapers or begging in the subway. Nonetheless, I had to do something quick because Misty and I had shared her *jelaba* in the last couple of days, and there was a chance that she had become infected as well.

Racking my brains, trying to come up with some quick moneymaking scheme, I finally settled on a second story job.

That night I watched and waited on Charles Street, lurking in doorways, clutching a short, sharp metal rod I had found on the pier. When the street was dark and quiet, I thrust the rod into my belt then ran up the stoop to the first floor of Misty's building. Standing on the handrail, I leaned out, reached for the ledge, pulled myself up, grasped the bars of the first-floor window, and hoisted myself onto the next ledge. I continued crawling up the wall like an ant, gripping it with my ragged fingernails and the rubber tread of my sneaker soles, until I had reached the fire escape on the second floor. Breathing hard, I paused, listening for some sign of discovery. But all was tranquil on Charles Street.

After that, there was nothing to it. I climbed swiftly and silently to the roof, slipped across to the roof next door, then kept going until I was four or five doors up the street. There, I crept down a rear fire escape past open windows and blaring television sets until I found an unlit, unbarred window on the fourth floor.

Waiting, breathing hard again, I listened until I was sure no one was home. Then I pulled the sharpened rod from my belt and punched it through the window just above the latch, making a small, jagged, hand-sized hole. The glass fell onto the ledge with a light tinkling sound, drowned out by tinny

TV laughter from the floor below. Listening again for any sign of discovery, I slipped the latch, levered the window slowly, silently upward a few inches, then squeezed through.

Inside, I threw a doily over a table lamp, switched it on low, latched the door chain to prevent surprise, and found myself in a small, crowded apartment with musty wall-to-wall carpeting, faded overstuffed furniture, yellowed photographs, stained brown wallpaper, green plastic light fixtures, and a low ceiling. Though the place was neat and the beds were made, it smelled of old people and dust lay thick on all the furniture.

Breathing easier, imagining its elderly residents in some shabby condominium on the West Coast of Florida, I searched the place for money and valuables. I went through the bedroom, bathroom, living room, guest bedroom, kitchen. Went through the closets, the bed clothing, and drawers. I searched under the furniture and above the shelves. But I found nothing. Not a penny. Not a strand of pearls. On the point of giving up, I thought of the refrigerator, where my Grandma Wasson used to keep her money. And there, in an old Mason jar, I found a crisp, cold, twenty-dollar bill.

"Awwwright!" I exclaimed aloud, shadowboxing around on the kitchen linoleum. Replacing the twenty with an IOU, I stripped and stuffed my crabby clothes in a plastic trash bag that I found under the kitchen sink. Then, dressed in a double-breasted suit that looked like it had not been worn since 1944, dragging the bag after me, I crawled out the window, climbed up the fire escape, then scampered across the roofs to Charles Street.

When Misty got home that night, I was waiting on her stoop. "What's with the antique suit?" she sniffed. "And the laundry bag?"

"Listen, Misty, I hate to tell you this, but . . ."

"You're kidding me, 'Nesto. Not *that!*"

"I'm sorry," I said, fishing in my bag for the big green bottle of Pyrinate 200. "But I got the cure."

"You better have, boy," she countered, though she did not appear to be much put out. In fact, she was already starting to laugh.

Like me, Misty had traveled the Great Grass Road to the East, and she had been through it all before.

Then inside her apartment, when we wanted to get into the shower and give each other the treatment, we discovered that the water had been shut off. Phoning upstairs to the neighbors, Misty learned that emergency repairs were being done and would not be completed until the next day.

"'Nesto, if you don't do something about this. . . ."

"Not to worry, love, I got just the place. . . ."

That night we climbed the stairs to the fifth floor, slipped through the trapdoor and out onto the rooftops. A few minutes later, inside the old folk's place, everything seemed exactly as I had left it. Stealthily, by the light of the doily-covered table lamp, we crept into the bathroom shower, turned on the hot water, shed our things, then hopped in together.

Giggling in the half-light, shaving our crotches and up under our arms, lathering the Pyrinate 200 over all smooth and slippery parts, we begin to grow aroused.

"Here, rub me here!" Misty panted. "Get those nasty things off me...."

"*Couch a hogshead with me then,*" the master said, "*in the darkmans clip and kiss.*"

We ended up on the floor in a pile of arms and legs, in a puddle of water, soapsuds and spent crabs.

Sated at last, shaved, rinsed, dried, parasite-free, fitted out in fresh 'Forties finery, we crept back through the apartment then tossed our dirty things into the courtyard below.

"*This* is the way I like you, 'Nesto!" Misty shouted in glee, as we clambered over the roofs in the darkness, with the lights of the metropolis in our eyes, the wind in our hair. "This is the way you were *meant* to be!"

Nevertheless, after the episode with the parasites, everything went back to normal on Charles Street. I slept alone, scratched my itchy stubble of sprouting pubic hair alone, whiled away ninety percent of my waking hours alone; and I had no illusions about how I would be spending the coming long Labor Day weekend.

All day Thursday and Friday that week I worked like a pack rat, begging in the subway, ransacking trash bins, collecting refundable bottles, selling them in supermarkets, stocking up on beans and rice, until I reckoned I had enough to hole up for the whole three days. On Friday night, I boiled the rice and beans, stirred them together in a giant pot, seasoned them with Misty's leftover spices and chili sauce, then dined at the kitchen counter amid the plants and fish tanks which had become my responsibility.

While the rest of New York City celebrated Labor Day weekend, I spent my days in peaceful contemplation. I browsed through Misty's science fiction library. I wrote in the last few pages of the journals that I had packed around the world. I listened to the top forty songs, most notably the Doors' "Light My Fire," and "Feelin' Groovy," by Harpers Bizarre, on Misty's portable radio, my tranquility disturbed only by some pushy reporter named Carla Brown phoning with urgent messages that I was made to copy verbatim and leave for Misty on her coffee table: "Can you please tell Ms. Thorssen that I'm a journalist seeking information about the death of a drug dealer named Bobby Franklin?"

Finally, on Sunday night, I was forced out of the apartment into the garden by the heat and the stench of my own bean farts. For some reason—maybe just because I wanted easy access to my journal—I brought my backpack along.

An hour or two before dawn, I was awakened by the sound of two muffled voices inside the apartment, one male, one female. The female sounded like Misty. The other sounded familiar, like someone from my distant past.

". . . fuckin' reporter . . ."

". . . lucky she came to us first, Misty . . ."

". . . boss finds out . . ."

". . . should've done her when . . ."

". . . do it now, Ray . . ."

". . . too late . . ."

For a minute or two, I lost the drift of the conversation, which until that point seemed quite casual in tone. When

I picked it up again, however, there was a pleading tone in Misty's voice.

"... who's Al to ..."

"... ain't just the crabs, Misty ..."

"... then what, Ray ..."

"... dis the boss ..."

"... friend of mine ..."

"... the fuck is he ..."

"... don't know ..."

"... lie to me ..."

Startled from my torpor by the sound of glass breaking, furniture falling over, a smothered cry, I considered heroics for an instant, but I had a sense that I might only make things worse for Misty.

All right, the truth is I was in such a panic that I could do nothing but make myself scarce.

Rolling off the deck chair, grabbing my rucksack, I slipped behind the bushes and over the mossy garden wall just as a man appeared at the French window.

A small, pot-bellied man of about fifty with a smudge of goatee and long dark hair pulled back in a ponytail, he switched on the outside light, slid the window open, then stepped out into the garden, breathing hard. His grey, hairy body, clad in a greasy T-shirt, stained pea-green Bermuda shorts, and dirty white loafers, gleamed with sweat. Tightly, tensely in his right hand, pointing downwards, he held a slender, silencer-equipped automatic pistol, which answered my unspoken question as to how he had so easily intimidated a strapping six-foot woman.

With his left hand, he reached for a soiled handkerchief to wipe his glittering eyes, his pointed snout, while swiveling his long, narrow head back and forth with the quick, twitching movements of a weasel searching the shadows for prey.

"The world is so fucking small!" I said to myself. Because I knew this guy! Granted, he had changed. When I met him, years before, hitching my way down through Central America, his hair was short, he had no beard, and he wore a pinstriped suit.

But how could anyone forget a rodent like Ray Minelli?

For an instant, I thought of jumping over the wall, stepping out in front of him, relying on the shock of my appearance and a reminder of our shared experiences on the road to appeal to his better instincts.

But then a healthy prudence intervened.

"You out there, man?" he demanded, in his high-pitched Brooklyn accent. Then, shaking his handkerchief rapidly back and forth rather daintily, he stuffed it into his back pocket. "Come on out, man. No one's gonna bite you, right?"

Misty appeared behind him, in a long, white, cotton dress of Mexican peasant design, ripped at the bodice. A stream of blood ran from her nose. Her eyes looked very round, very bright.

"'Nesto," she said, slipping past him into the garden. "If you're there, please come out."

Standing on the roof of somebody's old doghouse, peeking over the wall through the shrubbery, holding my breath, I went over my options, and decided that I had only one.

"Please," Misty repeated, in a quivery voice that was not her own, "he only wants to talk."

"Goddamnit, what is this shit? There's nobody out here," Ray sniffed. Then, he led Misty into the apartment and out of earshot again:

". . . big mistake, girl. . ."

". . . I swear. . ."

". . . knows too much, Misty. . ."

". . . you and me, Ray. . ."

". . . wag your tail at me. . ."

". . . begging you. . ."

". . . you think I like. . ."

The radio came on, very loud, Paul McCartney singing "Yesterday."

Then came a low bap-bap sound, like a couple of ladyfingers going off.

The music stopped.

"Sorry, sweetheart," said Ray, sobbing. "Bye-bye now."

The front door clicked shut.

Curled up on the dewy, tar paper roof of the doghouse on the other side of the garden wall, I tried to make sense of what had just happened. But there could be no doubt about what happened. The only question was whether to stick around to confirm a foregone conclusion or instantly disappear.

Across the garden I ran, over the wall, up the side of the house next-door like a human fly, up the fire escape, over the rooftops, down somebody else's fire escape, out onto Christopher Street.

If someone had called the police, they would be there in a minute. The precinct house was only three blocks away on West Tenth Street. And there was little doubt who the primary suspect would be.

Moi!

I did not cry for Misty. Already she was something other than herself. It was like . . . I'd had this flash before, the first minute I came to her door. In a way, she had been dead all along, and everything that happened in between was like a dream.

Down in the subway, I vaulted over the turnstile when the token clerk wasn't looking and caught a Number 3 Train uptown to 153rd Street and Amsterdam Avenue.

Emerging just as the sun came up, I strode briskly over the George Washington Bridge with my rucksack bouncing on my back, stopping only at a phone booth on the Jersey side to anonymously report a possible crime, including its probable motive, the name of the perp, and the name of his employer.

I never learned the outcome of the investigation. Never wanted to find out.

Shading my face from the sun, which was now directly in my eyes, I stood beside the westbound lane, just beyond the tollbooths, then hoisted my large hand-lettered sign toward the oncoming traffic:

"AROUND THE WORLD
BACKWARDS"

Chapter Eighteen

*A man travels the world
in search of what he needs
and returns home to find it.*
George Moore, 1916

Since this is to be my confession, as well as an account of my feverish life and loves, it is time for me now to correct the colorful impression which I have encouraged for many years, which indeed I came to believe myself, that like the great explorers of old I circled the entire globe, and that I did it backwards.

Though I did, in fact, cross most of the earth's landmass, and much of its watery surface as well, and I most definitely did it backwards, I missed, to my everlasting regret, that vast, empty stretch of Pacific Ocean between Japan and Hawaii. However, I have flown over its expanse many times in the decades since then.

Whatever the technicalities, seven years after I set out blithely for the Mexican border, I reached my native shores again (riding an empty Western Pacific freight car across the Sierra Nevada from Reno), with the egregious misapprehension that I was "a sadder and wiser man."

The late sixties were wild times in the Bay Area, and the year I arrived was no exception.

Nevertheless, I firmly resolved in my journal on that first golden day in San Francisco, (mixing metaphors as usual), "*to keep my nose to the grindstone, for my oats have already been well sown.*"

Then, to give my resolution the imprimatur I felt it deserved, I quoted an obscure passage from the master, which may or may not have been relevant: "*Cypherjuggles going the highroads, wild oats to mum.*"

Several months before, while still in Japan, I had applied for graduate school at the San Francisco State University Writer's Workshop. Upon arrival, I found to my delight that I had not only been accepted, but that *Samsara*, the short story I'd sent in with my application, based on my relationship with Masako, had won me a partial scholarship as well.

Even better, the first installment was awaiting me in the bursar's office. With the scholarship money, I rented a one-bedroom apartment, a third-floor walk-up in the Haight-Ashbury District, and stocked its larder with rice and beans. Through the college's employment agency, I got a night job as a janitor at the American Heart Association, starting immediately.

On the first day of school, standing in a line of a hundred graduate students outside the Writer's Workshop offices, waiting for a session with my advisor, killing time with a paperback edition of Andre Malraux's *Man's Fate*," I came upon these words:

> "He needed the eyes of others to see himself,
> the senses of another to feel himself."

I scribbled them down on the inside of the cover. Then two things occurred to me at once. First, I had no friends in San Francisco, where I would be spending the next year or two at least. Second, I was standing in a veritable marketplace of pulchritudinous young females, so it was essential to shop fast before all the good ones were snapped up.

Begging the irritable, overweight young woman behind me to save my place, I took a stroll up and down the winding queue to brazenly view the merchandise. After one long, slow circuit I found the choices so appealing that I was hard put to make a selection. After another amble to the front of the file and back, I had narrowed it down to a blue-eyed blond with the cheery demeanor and the All-American good looks of a high school cheerleader, versus a tall, dark, sultry brunette. After another quick tour, I fixed on the sloe-eyed girl. And not merely for her lush Mediterranean beauty, or the intelligence and complexity in her countenance, or the extraordinary length of the black Nat Sherman cigarette she was smoking. What fascinated me most, I think, was that she was dressed in a tweed business suit, a crisp, white blouse, and high heeled shoes. Virtually everyone else was in hippy garb, of which I had seen, worn, and smelled enough on the Great Grass Road to last a lifetime.

My next step was to think of a line to feed her. Unable to come up with anything original on a moment's notice, I decided on the direct approach.

"Hey, I know those Nat Shermans cost a fortune," I said, sauntering up to her, flashing a grin. "But can I bum one off you? I swear I'll return the favor."

She grinned back and replied, "Well, why not then?"

When she offered me one from the pack, I waited to see whether she would light it for me, whether she would cup her fingers around mine when she did.

Imagine my feverish delight when . . .

"Where you from?" I asked when she'd lit me up. "Don't tell me. Let me guess. New York, right?"

"Oh shit! You could tell from just four words?"

"I know you've worked on it, dear, but there's still a little Queens or Long Island in there somewhere."

"Damn, you've found me out!" she snorted. "It's Queens. What about you?"

"Originally L.A.," I replied. "But I've just spent the last seven years hitchhiking around the world . . . backwards."

That grabbed her, as I knew it would. Right away she wanted to know all about my trip. As I briefly filled her in, I noted that she had written six tentative course numbers on a pad she was carrying, and I instantly committed them to memory. I even went so far as to calculate which four of the six she was most likely to take, and which of those were probably oversubscribed.

"Sorry, I've got to get back if I want to keep my place in line," I said, after I had consumed only half the cigarette. And I was delighted to confirm that she was perhaps a bit disappointed to see me leave.

"Hey, what's your name?" she wanted to know.

"Ernesto Brawley," I said, trilling the "R" in Ernesto. "And yours?"

"Marina."

"Marina what? Wait. Don't tell me. Lemme guess. It's Italian, right?"

"Right again!" she laughed. "It's Marina Belforte."

"Well, okay, Marina, see you then," I said, then quickly added, *"Ciao, bella! Ci vediamo subito, non?"*

"Ma cierto, Ernesto, ciao!" she replied, beaming with pleasure at my idiomatic exercise of her ancestral tongue. "For sure we'll run into each other around here someplace, right?"

But she had no idea how sure.

On the first day of school, I was in her morning short story class. "Nice to see you again," she said, smiling, taking a seat beside me. That afternoon, when Marina walked into her modern novel class, she spotted me right away in the back row and slid in next to me again.

"Hey, Ernesto, this is getting to be a habit!"

"No shit!"

Then the next day, in her creative writing class, there I was again. "Wow, this can't be real!" she tittered, shaking her curly black trusses. "I suppose you're enrolled in my Russian literature course too, right?"

"Right."

"This is just the most incredible series of coincidences!"

"Hey, they are not coincidences, Marina," I said, echoing a line I'd fed to another Italian girl, Fausta, years before.

"No? What are they, then?"

"È *destino!*" I cried, with all the fervor in my lying heart, and she fell out.

As it transpired, Marina was not nearly as conventional as she had appeared in the beginning, and her personality was full of contradictions.

Over the next weeks of class, I discovered that she was a bright, even brilliant literature student, and a talented writer, but she had a fiery, Italian temperament. Touchy, easy to anger, she took herself very, very seriously indeed. She was afraid of absolutely no one, least of all our professors, whom she challenged at every opportunity. She criticized other students' work with brutal candor but accepted no criticism of her own. On the other hand, despite all evidence to the contrary, she distrusted her emotions and made valiant attempts to maintain strict control over herself. This was evident in her writing, where she weaved keen, complex insights and observations into a fastidious, circumlocutory, almost Jamesian narrative style that absolutely went against the grain of the time.

Perhaps the most surprising aspect of Marina's contradictory character, which she admitted to me only after weeks of collegial fellowship, was that she had a night job as a topless waitress. She worked at Goman's Gay Sixties, a club on Broadway in North Beach that featured a nude trampoline act, and a huge streetlamp out front with a live, half-naked, dancing girl inside. There was even a topless picture of Marina on the marquee outside, and I never passed by the place without having a quick gander at her marmoreal Mediterranean breasts.

Yet, there was another side of Marina that was still just a Catholic schoolgirl from Bellrose, Queens—honest, virtuous, diligent, and *very* careful with men. She suffered no illusions, had little tolerance for jive, distrusted all dreams and rosy scenarios. But she sincerely believed in a conventional God figure. She even had a soft, squishy spot for some of the more implausible teachings of the Church of Rome.

As for myself, Marina did not altogether trust me, for good reason. I strove long, mightily, and deviously to get a date with her. Yet, she resisted my advances until I wrote a short story called *The Walls of Sicily* for our creative writing class.

The plot concerned an American World War II veteran who gets a divorce then goes back to find the Sicilian girl he loved when he was a young soldier. It was a true story that I heard from an old GI who picked me up when I was hitchhiking in Italy, but I contrived to paint the Sicilian girl in colors that evoked Marina's appearance, personality, and character, couching them in the most flattering terms. So flattering, in fact, that the one thing our professor, Leo Litwak, criticized about the story was "its fatal tendency to romanticize the girl."

After passionately defending the character of the girl, and arguing Professor Litwak into exhausted submission, Marina approached me after class, calling out, "*Bravo, Ernesto, stupendo!* No matter what Leo or anyone else says, it's one of the most beautiful love stories I've ever read!"

It was then that Marina chose to extend to me, for the first time, the privilege of accompanying her on the streetcar to her studio apartment on Fillmore Street. She invited me in for coffee, and I was touched by the place's lack of amenities. Though clean and neat, it was entirely empty save for a table and chairs in the kitchen, a mattress on the floor of the main room and a stack of books in the corner. The only thing that enlivened it was a little, white kitten that came meowing to the door when we stepped inside.

"Hey, what's your name, buddy?" I asked, stooping down to pet it.

"It's a girl," Marina said. "And I think I'm going to call her Sicily."

"Flattery will get you everywhere," I quipped, quoting my old Thai love, rather pathetically in retrospect, yet Marina laughed long and loud.

Even so, she would not let me get near that mattress on her floor. She seated me instead at her kitchen table, where she engaged me in a lengthy literary conversation.

"You know, I want us to be really good friends!" she called after me as I was leaving for work.

"Is that all we can be?"

"Oh, come on, Ernesto."

"No, really, I'd like to know."

"What are you saying, precisely?" Marina snapped, her Italian flaring up. "That you're *interested* in me? You want to have *a scene* with me? If that's so, I can't imagine why, other than just some sexual trip. Apart from literature, what do we have in common? You revel in risk, adventure, the unknown, mysteries of all kinds. I loathe all that kind of shit. You glory in the outdoors, and I hate hiking, camping, picnicking, anything without sidewalks. You are Mr. Coordination. I can't dance, swim, ride a bike, drive a car, or play any sport. If you want to know the full truth, I suffer from nearly every known phobia, including claustrophobia and acrophobia. The only thing I am not afraid of is people, especially stuffed shirts. There's nothing I like better than cutting them down to size. You on the other hand are easygoing, deferential. You'll do anything to avoid a fight. In class, you let everyone walk all over you. You won't even defend yourself when you're obviously in the right. We are so different, Ernesto! I doubt if any two people could be more different. Now don't give me any shit about 'opposites attract.'"

"All right, what are you really trying to tell me, Marina?" I sneered. "That you've got a boyfriend?"

"Well..." she replied, laughing, lightening up. "Among other things, yes."

"Who is he? No, let me guess. Your old professor?"

"Jesus, you are uncanny, man," Marina said, shaking her head. "How'd you figure that one out?

"It's written all over you," I retorted. "You said it yourself. Fear of risk. He's probably married, devoted to his family, old enough to be your father. You probably don't even get to see him that much, so there's no danger of anything long-term or too serious. Also, maybe you had some trouble with your old man, a hard-ass Neapolitan, when you were a kid. This is your kind of... 'compensation.' The daddy you never had. Am I right?"

"Uh, more or less, if you must reduce something infinitely complicated to its most simplistic terms," she replied, blushing for the first time in our acquaintance. "He was my poetry professor at Berkeley. We still see each other whenever we get a chance."

"Okay, I can dig that," I tossed off.

"Does that mean we can still be friends?"

"Hey, it's automatic," I said, turning to go.

But I resolved then to never flag or fail until I had won Marina Belforte's Italian heart.

In January, during the winter break, she took a week off from her waitress job and flew down to meet her poet at a spa in Tecate, Mexico.

Consumed by jealousy, I worked it out by writing a short story entitled *The Horned Toad* in which a disconsolate graduate student named Dirty Ernie dresses himself in a horned toad suit and drives a 1949 Ford called the Jungle Cruiser all the way to Tecate, Mexico, in search of his lost love.

When Marina returned, and I showed her the story, she laughed and said, "You know, it's funny. The part where you crouch in the trees in your horned toad suit and spy on the lovers while they're making love in the hot tub? That really happened, and all the time I was thinking, '*What if Ernesto is out there somewhere?*'"

"You think of me when you're making love with another guy?"

"Sometimes."

"I'll win you in the end; you know that don't you, Marina?"

"I wouldn't bet on it," she said, smiling, shaking her head.

And for more than a year and a half, it seemed that she would have her way. We were study mates, literary fellows, friends, and confidants, but nothing more.

Near the end of our course of studies at San Francisco State, we were invited to a graduation party at a classmate's house in Sausalito. Having just won a literary prize, I was the guest of honor. Toward the end when, under the influence of a half-liter of Sonoma jug-wine, I sang a heartfelt *cante jondo* to a Spanish friend's inspired flamenco guitar, topping it off with a gypsy toe and heel, I saw for the first time in Marina's eyes an ardent possibility—of which I had only dared dream until then.

We had both secured teaching jobs, Marina at the University of Oregon, and I at the University of Hawaii. It was late July, and we were packing to leave. We arranged to meet and say our goodbyes at a little coffee shop on upper Fillmore Street, near her apartment.

"Well, girl, I guess this is it!" I said, shaking my head.

"Yes, I . . . guess so."

"Anything you regret?"

"I . . . I suppose there is," she murmured.

Then, for the first time, I saw the formidable Marina Belforte's bottom lip begin to tremble.

"If you could do it all over again," I said, looking her in the eye. "What would you do, Marina?"

"No question," she responded, as a tear ran down her cheek. "I'd marry you in a minute."

"All right," I said, trying hard not to betray my feelings of exultation, vindication, and triumph. "Let's do it then!"

So, Marina phoned in her regrets to the University of Oregon, and to her ex-professor at Berkeley. I said goodbye to the little eighteen-year-old I'd been dating, and we had a big, last-minute wedding in a friend's old Maybeck house in Bolinas.

There was a rock band, Indian food, and prodigious amounts of liquor. All our family members, friends, and classmates attended. A local counterculture Unitarian minister, sporting high heeled boots, bellbottom corduroys, a fluffy, white blouse with the neck open to show his hairy chest, performed the honors. Marina stood beside me in a long, white, linen dress, hand-painted by a Bolinas artist with abstract splotches of blue and black, and she was impossibly beautiful. Her long, wavy, jet-black hair glowed in the California sunlight. Her dark eyes, full of tears, were enormous, with heavy lids and lashes. The shape of her face was aquiline, with a gently curving nose like my mother's, but her lips were much fuller, her neck longer, her skin darker. Whether perceived or imagined, the resemblance warmed my soul, filled me with a sense of rightness, of well-being, a sense that *"Sumer is icumen in, Lhude sing cuccu!"* It was the fever, yes, but not the raging, short-lived fever I had known in the past. It was a calm, clement fever, one that soothed rather than burned, comforted rather than tormented. It was the pleasure I had felt as a small child home from school with a temperature, chewing Asper gum, with a whole day of my yet sober Mama's undivided solicitude to look forward to. The fever that makes you kick your feet under the covers with delight. The fever you want to last forever.

In this confession, I have spoken of many women. But you, Marina Belforte, you are the love of my life.

Chapter Nineteen

*I tend to live in the past
Because most of my life is there.*
Herb Caen

Now, as we come to the end of this long stretch of Fever Road, I feel compelled to at least make a brief attempt to sum up my experience, much as I hate to philosophize. The question I feel obliged to answer now is this: Was there any wisdom to be found in my mad, impetuous, unfinished passage about the world? Did I gain anything significant during my gene-driven, fever-ridden journey?

And my answer is, "Yes, absolutely. I learned something vital." My lesson was this: There is nothing to be learned on the Fever Road. Nothing, that is, that one could not have learned in a more tranquil mode. Unfortunately, however, the only way to reach that profound conclusion, and disabuse oneself of illusion, is by putting a lot of road under one's belt.

As always, my infallible guide and master, James Joyce, has the last word on the subject.

> *We walk through ourselves,*
> *meeting robbers, ghosts, giants,*
> *old men, young men, wives, brothers-in-love.*
> *But always meeting ourselves.*

And what of all my romantic adventures? Did I learn anything from them? Only one thing, but something which has permanently shaped my insight into the nature of reality:

The universe is a perfect ovum, governed strictly by the female principle.

End of story.
It's all a game.

www.ingramcontent.com/pod-product-compliance
Lightning Source LLC
Chambersburg PA
CBHW030137170426
43199CB00008B/104